Journey of the Wounded Soul: Poetic Companions for Spiritual Struggles

Louis Hoffman, PhD
Steve Fehl, PsyD
Editors

Colorado Springs, CO
www.universityprofessorspress.com

Book Copyright © 2016
The authors of the poems retain the copyright for all poems in this book.

Journey of the Wounded Soul: Poetic Companions for Spiritual Struggles
By Louis Hoffman and Steve Fehl

All rights reserved. No portion of this book may be reproduced by any process or technique without the express written consent of the publishers.

First Published in 2016. University Professors Press. United States.

ISBN 13: 978-1-939686-13-8

University Professors Press
Colorado Springs, CO
www.universityprofessorspress.com

Front Photo by Louis Hoffman
Cover Design by Laura Ross

This volume does a masterful job of describing the true depth of life experience through poetic verse. Readers who may feel utterly alone in their misery will experience companionship and understanding. In a unique way, they will be helped to "make it through the night" (in the words of Willie Nelson's classic song). While they will still know the truth of the old spiritual, "You have to walk the lonesome highway all alone; nobody else can walk it for you," they will yet sense others are walking it, too. This book is a valuable contribution in both theory and therapy.

H. Newton Malony, PhD
Author, *Religion in the History of Psychology*

Try reading each of the poems in this marvelous collection by therapists and clients, academics and students, poets and novices, who have advocated for the inclusion of the humanities in their theories, research, practice, and lives. *Journey of the Wounded Soul* is a collection of poems that bears testament to the human condition. Each of these carefully chosen selections tells its own story. Each can be read—and read again—to provide insight, compassion, and inspiration.

Stanley Krippner, PhD
Alan Watts Professor of Psychology, Saybrook University
Co-author, *Personal Mythology*, Co-editor, *Healing Stories*

In this book, *Journey of the Wounded Soul: Poetic Companions for Spiritual Struggles*, authors Louis Hoffman and Steve Fehl do something extraordinary. They provide us with companionship as well as poetic license to share our own spiritual struggles and to find the gold hidden in these struggles. These struggles, that include existential loneliness, doubting, and questioning, are often best expressed through the arts. When discursive language fails, symbolism, image, and rhythm can sometimes convey more powerfully the depths life's struggle. It is difficult and lonely to be a genuine seeker. By providing this book of thoughts and poems, Hoffman and Fehl give us permission to share our own struggles as well.

Ilene Serlin, PhD
Author, *Whole Person Healthcare*

Journey of the Wounded Soul helps you take off the familiar glasses that frame your life and open you up to different ways of experiencing. These poems enable you to take suffering by the hand and walk with it as you might with an old friend. There are no empty promises in this book but just an open and honest invitation to walk with suffering wherever it leads. The *Journey of the Wounded Soul* is challenging, wise, and surprisingly hopeful.

Glendon Moriaty, PsyD
Professor, Regent University
Author, *Pastoral Care of Depression* and *Integrating Faith and Psychology*

The beauty inherent in this gem of a book is embodied in the way it organically weaves the thread of spirituality through the terrible and sublime, through sadness and joy, through grief and illumination, and through despair and hope. It celebrates the paradox and mystery of spirituality and provides raw, rare, precious glimpses into the heart of healing that is usually such a private, solitary experience. I am deeply grateful for these courageous offerings. I look forward to using this book in my work with clients in their own journeys through trauma and loss and the recovery of spirituality. I also plan to gift my therapist colleagues as a boon for their own personal and professional journeys.

Drake Spaeth, PsyD
Associate Professor, Chicago School of Professional Psychology
Adjunct Faculty, Saybrook University
Ordained Minister, Earth Traditions

Dedication

This book is dedicated to my wife, Heatherlyn Hoffman. It troubles my heart that it is not until my 8th book that I dedicate one to you. Each book that came out did not rise to a level adequate to reflect my love for you. I realize now that no book filled with words could be worthy enough to dedicate to you. It is fitting that I overcome my unworthiness with this book and dedicate it to you. In my love for you I have experienced a love that is a testament that something greater exists. In your love I have found beauty that overwhelms and mystifies me day after day. If this is not the heart of spirituality, I likely will never find it. With all my heart and all my love, I dedicate this book to you.

~ Louis Hoffman

This book is dedicated to my wife, Christine Ray. For almost thirty years you have stood by me and with me in the midst of pain, loss, doubt, fear, failure, and struggle. You have helped me not only understand unconditional love and unending grace, but through you I have experienced both. Throughout all the ups and downs over the years you have given me dedication, faithfulness, forgiveness, honesty, a generous spirit, and unrelenting tenderness. This book is only one small way in which I can express my love for you, as well as the thankfulness I have for all the ways you have blessed my life. I love you so much!

~ Steve Fehl

Poetry, Healing, and Growth Book Series

Stay Awhile: Poetic Narratives on Multiculturalism and Diversity
Louis Hoffman & Nathaniel Granger, Jr. (Eds.)

Capturing Shadows: Poetic Encounters Along the Path of Grief and Loss
Louis Hoffman & Michael Moats (Eds.)

Journey of the Wounded Soul: Poetic Companions for Spiritual Struggles
Louis Hoffman & Steve Fehl (Eds.)

The Last Walk: Using Poetry for Grieving and Remembering Our Pets
Louis Hoffman, Michael Moats, and Tom Greening (Eds.)
(Summer, 2016)

Connoisseurs of Suffering: Poetry for the Journey to Meaning
Jason Dias and Louis Hoffman (Fall, 2016)

Lullabies and Confessions: Poetic Explorations of Parenting Across the Lifespan
Louis Hoffman and Lisa Vallejos
(Fall, 2016)

Silent Screams: Poetic Journeys with Addiction and Recovery
Nathaniel Granger, Jr. and Louis Hoffman (Winter, 2017)

Poetry, Healing, and Growth Series

Poetry is an ancient healing art used across cultures for thousands of years. In the Poetry, Healing, and Growth book series, the healing and growth-facilitating nature of poetry is explored in depth through books of poetry and scholarship, as well as through practical guides on how to use poetry in the service of healing and growth. Poetry written with an intention to transform suffering into an artistic encounter is often different in process and style from poetry written for art's sake. In this series, there is engagement with the poetic greats and literary approaches to poetry while also embracing the beauty of fresh, poetic starts and encouraging readers to embark upon their own journey with poetry. Whether you are an advanced poet, avid consumer, or novice to poetry, we are confident you will find something to inspire your thinking or your personal path toward healing and growth.

Series Editors,
Carol Barrett, PhD, Steve Fehl, PsyD, Nathaniel Granger, Jr, PsyD, Tom Greening, PhD, and Louis Hoffman, PhD

Table of Contents

Acknowledgements	i
Foreword by Thomas Moore	vii
Introduction	1
Waiting for the Blessing – Louis Hoffman	27
Always Sunset – Steve Fehl	29
Passeggiata with Saint Francis – Lorraine Mangione	31
Coal Town Hospice – Robert A. Neimeyer	33
Manufracture – Richard Bargdill	35
A Simple Game with Stones – Sean Gunning	36
A Little Sesshin to Soothe My Soul – Virginia (Gina) Subia Belton	38
Leaves – Glenn Graves	39
Preparing for My Medicine Dance – Candice Hershman	40
Drawing an Angel – Carol Barrett	41
A Very Thin Line – Paul T. P. Wong	42
"Potter to the Pot about the Wheel" – Ted Mallory	44
The Struggle – Nathaniel Granger, Jr.	45
False Prophets – Nesreen (Alsoraimi) Frost	46
Ode to a Teenage Life – Steve Fehl	48
A Feral Innocence – LeesaMaree Bleicher	49
Not Even Tinsel – Lorraine Mangione	50
Something in Those Blue Eyes – Louis Hoffman	51
Colorado to New Hampshire – Lorraine Mangione	53
Blessed End; Sorrowful Beginning – Rodger E. Broomé	55
Inevitability – Tamiko Lemberger-Truelove	56
Last Christmas – Hajnalka Kurti Woosley	57
Panning – Robert A. Neimeyer	59
Silent Night – Jyl Anais Ion	61
The End of Self – Tamiko Lemberger-Truelove	62
Filing a Soul Exemption – Candice Hershman	63
Animal & Angel – David Bentata	66
The Human Legacy – Monir Saleh	68
In Praise of Sheep – B. M. Lyon	69
No Samaritan – Sean Gunning	70
Grant Me a Second Chance, Lord – Paul T. P. Wong	73

Redemption – David N. Elkins	74
The Human Condition – Emily Lasinsky	75
Starving Children – Wade Agnew	76
Preacher Man – Louis Hoffman	77
Falling for Fall – Kristen Beau Howard	78
Nature's Refuge – Larry Graber	79
Autumn – Steve Fehl	83
Saint Fido – Dan Hocoy	84
Medicine Woman – Juanita Ratner	85
Simpler Times (A Cantankerous Old Man's Perspective) – Nathaniel Granger, Jr.	86
A Path? – Tom Greening	87
Idea of Reference – Hans Cox	88
Checkmates and Exes – Nesreen (Alsoraimi) Frost	89
Day by Day – Sean Gunning	91
On Hadrian's Wall – B. M. Lyon	92
First Religion – David Bentata	93
Pilgrimage – Carol Barrett	95
All Souls' Day – Lorraine Mangione	97
My Quiet Place/Further Meditations on My Quiet Place – Larry Graber	98
The Call of the Search – Shelley Pizzuto	101
The Anti-Christ – Candice Hershman	102
silly little buddha – Banu Ibaoglu Vaughn	104
Collecting Christian Sentiments – Louis Hoffman	105
Be Still – Michael E. Moats	107
I Pray for Scars *for my sister* – Richard Bargdill	111
An Empty Soul – Steve Fehl	113
Sacrifice at Eleven Years Old – Erica Loberg	115
Taking the Prayers Back – Candice Hershman	117
Lost and Found – Emily Lasinsky	120
Made in the Image – Dakota Gundy	121
Prayer – Edward Korber	123
Prayer in Poetry – Yasna C. Provine	125
In the Trenches – Sean Gunning	127
Absolute – Tracy Lee Sisk	129
Oh, How I Wish – Steve Fehl	130
Soul Sisters – Nesreen (Alsoraimi) Frost	131
Revelation – Nick Owen	132
Nurturer of Spirits – Natalia Mello	135
Strangers – Michelle Sideroff	138

Abhidharma – Katherine Kreil-Sarkar	139
Already Lost – Jyl Anais Ion	140
In Darkness Lives… - Lorraine Mangione	142
It's Personal – Nathaniel Granger, Jr.	144
The Stars Speak – Erica Palmer	146
Autobiography – Keaneasha Garcia	147
Perpetual Motion – Kat V. Rosemond	149
"Immaculate Combustion" – Joshua Ferguson	153
Spirituality – David Bentata	154
Spirit and Stardust – Carrie Arnold	155
Temptation – Carol Barrett	156
Prayer – Matthew D. Eayre	157
Life is a Contradiction in Terms – Richard Bargdill	158
Moon Half-Full – Sean Gunning	163
Life – Steve Fehl	165
Of Ashes and of Dirt – Tamiko Lemberger-Truelove	166
Stranger – Nesreen (Alsoraimi) Frost	167
The Addict – Juanita Ratner	169
Blend – Emily Lasinsky	173
Transcendence is Not the Way… - Candice Hershman	175
Supplication – Katherine Kreil-Sarkar	177
The Dahlia – Nance Reynolds	178
Eyes – Louis Hoffman	179
Send-off – Robert A. Neimeyer	181
Invocation – Lorraine Mangione	183
Here – Jyl Anais Ion	184
Equanimity – Bruce Elliot Alford	185
When a Student is Ready – Wade Agnew	186
Appendix – Poetry Activities	189
About the Editors	193

Acknowledgements:
Appreciation with a Message

First, we would like to thank the many people who contributed poems to this volume. To be so vulnerable is a gift. We hope you know how deeply we value the gift you offered in sharing your poems with us. We would also like to acknowledge the people who submitted poems that were not accepted. It was difficult to decide which ones to include in such a vast array of submissions. We reviewed many touching poems that did not get included in this book.

    We would also like to thank Joy Hoffman, who reviewed a number of poems, helping us make our final decisions. Our appreciation also goes to Susan Cooper for her expert editorial assistance. Additionally, we are deeply grateful Thomas Moore agreed to write the Foreword for this volume. We are also appreciative of his encouragement and support for this project. Few others have examined spirituality and the related struggles with as much depth and sensitivity as Moore, as is evident in his Foreword.

    We would like to thank University Professors Press and their board of editors who have enthusiastically supported the development of a series of books on poetry, healing, and growth. At a time when we read regularly about the death of the humanities, it is courageous for a small scholarly press to recognize the value of poetry in an academic context.

Each time I (Louis) sit down to write an acknowledgement section, I am deeply humbled by all the people who helped make the book a reality. I normally write these sections with tears and hope that people will read the acknowledgements along with the rest of the book. The journey of creating a book is a beautiful experience, yet one that comes with many sacrifices along the way. Having embarked on a number of poetry books lately, I have become acutely aware of the blessings as well as the costs. There is never time in my busy work schedule for such endeavors, so I pay for these in the hours I should be sleeping. Yet, the rewards from these projects have covered the cost. It is generally one's family who pays the most yet are often unrecognized when the book comes out. Without the love, support, and patience of my wife, Heatherlyn, and my sons, Lakoda, Lukaya, and Lyon, I could never write a book. I thank them and I hope that everyone who reads this book knows that they are just as essential a part of it as I am. They deserve to have their names on the cover just as much as I do.

My parents, Lynn and Clarence Hoffman, have always supported me in my spiritual journey, even though I know it has caused them worry and discomfort at times. But Mom and Dad—really, I'm okay. It is hard to embrace one's spiritual struggles as part of a spiritual journey without having a foundation. For me, my family has been a big part of that foundation. Without you, my spirituality would likely appear much stronger while in reality be built upon a fragile foundation. Through your support, I have been able to find something much deeper and more meaningful than I would have otherwise. I would also like to thank many others in my family who have been a spiritual support: my brother and sister-in-law, John and Joy Hoffman; my mother-in-law, Helen Rahming; and my father and mother-in-law, Earnal and Stephanie Cleare.

I also need to give a special acknowledgement to my good friend Glen Moriarty. We have often shared our struggles, including spiritual struggles, with each other. Glen has always showed a profound acceptance of me at each phase of my spiritual journey, but from within that acceptance he has also challenged me when I needed it. Glen, your friendship has been a blessing to me personally and spiritually.

There are many friends who deserve special credit with this book, but in particular John Johnson. When I was at a crossroads in my spirituality and experienced my most difficult dark night, it was Johnny who provided an encouragement that changed my life. I am sure he does not even know the depths of how much this impacted me. While suffering and deeply discouraged with myself, it was Johnny who told me that "wrestling with God" was my spiritual gift. The seeds of this book were planted with those words, and I am ever grateful. There are many other friends and mentors who have been a deep blessing on my spiritual journey: Paul Vasconcellos, a theology professor in my undergraduate program who taught it was okay to doubt; Eric Reither, a friend who was instrumental as I began questioning aspects of what I had been taught about religion; John Sharp, who, though we frequently disagreed, persevered through many hours of theological conversations and tolerated my constant wrestling with theology; Clarence Leung, Elizabeth Thompson, Brad Robison, Jonathon Choi, Audrey Khatchikian, John Johnson (again),

Acknowledgements

Tesi Athens, and Matt Bush, who were all part of a study group at Fuller Seminary where we often debated theology while supporting each other in our spiritual journeys; H. Newton Malony, my mentor and professor in graduate school who modeled spiritual questioning and dialogue beautifully; Jay Gattis, a friend whom I used to meet with weekly, often discussing our spiritual journeys; Robert J. Murney, who was a mentor and friend in my professional and spiritual development; Emory Cowan, who modeled a different type of faith and always supported my spirituality and my life journey.

I must include two acknowledgements that many may find strange. First, I need to thank my dogs, Amaya and Dante. Dogs have been an important part of my spirituality, which many will find odd, but a few will resonate with. Amaya and Dante have often helped keep me spiritually connected. Second, I wish to acknowledge the Colorado mountains, which provide spiritual and aesthetic inspiration on a daily basis. Returning to Colorado has been a spiritual blessing to me and has helped me to finish my portion of this book.

I would also like to thank many friends who have always remained supportive and instrumental in my development as a writer: Mark Yang, Xuefu Wang, Brittany Garrett-Bowser, Steve Pritzker, Michael Moats, Nathaniel Granger, Jr., Jason Dias, Shawn Rubin, Theopia Jackson, Dan Hocoy, Jim Ungvarsky, Susan Cooper, Kirk Schneider, Ed Mendelowitz, Myrtle Heery, and Willson Williams.

I, too, would like to give an acknowledgement to many students over the years who have taken an interest in poetry and its role in the healing process. You have been an inspiration to me and helped keep me motivated to write.

Last, I want to acknowledge Steve Fehl, my partner on this book. We came from similar religious backgrounds and followed similar paths. I have very fond memories of many hours of conversations about spirituality and religion. Your courage to wrestle with faith is inspiring, and I know that courage blesses many others more than you will ever know. It is deeply meaningful to me to collaborate on such an important project.

Like Louis, I (Steve) am acutely aware that there are many, many people who have been a part of my process of spiritual struggle and faith journey, many of whom will never see their name in print. I am also aware of the many people who have invited me into their spiritual journeys and allowed me to walk beside them as we wrestled with faith questions and experiences relating to that which is greater than ourselves. To each of you I say thank you for your presence, participation, and sharing in this difficult, yet meaningful struggle of accepting and striving to understand the power of spirituality in your life and mine. The lack of your name's presence in no way diminishes your significance in my spiritual trek!

As Louis said earlier, often the ones who go most unrecognized when undertaking projects such as this are those closest to us. First and foremost among this group is my wife, Chris. Her patience, tolerance, dedication, encouragement, and unconditional acceptance of me throughout our almost 30 years together are beyond my comprehension, and it is so inadequate to say the words 'thank you,' but I do thank you from the bottom of my heart and soul. In addition, I want to acknowledge my step-daughter, Joanne Baclig Price, and my three grandchildren Mason, Destiny, and Elijah. Your presence in my life, as well as your acceptance of me as a parent and grandparent touch me in ways I cannot describe in words. I also wish to acknowledge my three brothers and their wives. Barry and Colleen, Scott and Jane, and Chrys and Debbie, I am deeply thankful for all the love and support you have offered me throughout the myriad of transitions I have experienced. I love all of you very much!

It is rare that one makes a friend who is steadfast over the years and decades. My college roommate, Kent Mathews, is one of those rare individuals. Today, we meet every Friday for lunch and share what is happening in our lives, as well as discuss the many questions we encounter on our individual spiritual journeys. Kent, I would never have guessed that forty years after graduating from college we would still enjoy such a close bond. Thank you for your listening ear, your challenging perspectives, your intellectual tenacity, and your caring heart.

Another individual who has been a major part of my spiritual journey is Steven Arnold. I first met him after graduating from college and over the years he has been a friend and mentor, who provided spiritual guidance, honest and direct feedback, prayerful and meditative compassion and care, as well as incredible knowledge and insight. Thank you for walking with me as I wrestled with growing in maturity as a person and as a person of faith.

There are many others who need to be mentioned, but the space is limited. However, there are some individuals whom I wish to thank for the indelible mark they have left on my life and soul. Professors Robert Connors and Marvin Bergman were undergraduate professors who patiently listened to my quandaries, and encouraged me to engage with my spiritual questions. Throughout my professional career there have been individuals who appeared at just those moments when their wisdom was needed. They include Rod Boriack, Cindy Wheeler, Jim Ollhoff, Patra Pfotenhauer-Mueller, Stacy Tassler-Crosson, Christin Gregory, Jason Diaz, and Erica Palmer. Thank you for your presence and invaluable perspectives.

Over the last several years there have been a couple of groups that have played major roles in my spiritual struggles. The first group is one with which I began training in *Unearthing the Moment*. We continue to meet on an annual basis, and our times together have provided me some of the most significant spiritual experiences in my life. The group is led by Myrtle Henry, a wonderfully frank, wise, and compassionate teacher and facilitator. The group members who push me and embrace me include Stacy Aquipel, Kate Calhoon, Cathy Calvert, Thea Comeau, Debye Galaska, and Christopher Grimes. Each September I eagerly anticipate our time together and the conversations that stimulate my thinking and remind me that my questions are worthy of the wrestling with which I engage. Thank you!

A second is a group of friends who meet once a month to explore various forms of spirituality from Native American practices to Eastern thought to tarot cards. Thank you for giving me the permission and freedom to wonder aloud and challenge my world view concerning spirituality, faith, and the universe.

Finally, this list would not be complete without acknowledging my partner on this project – Louis Hoffman. I first met Louis ten years ago as I was working on my doctorate. At the time of our first meeting, I was not just struggling with questions of faith, religion, and spirituality; but in addition, I was wondering if I truly fit into the current psychology movement. My affection for and interest in existential-humanistic psychology seemed outdated and that I was a dinosaur in the evolution of psychological theories and methodologies. Louis was willing to sit, listen, and guide me, encouraging me to really engage with my questions and ponderings concerning psychology and faith. Particularly meaningful was discovering that we shared a great deal of similarities in our religious up-bringing. Louis's mentoring, teaching, openness, and vulnerability have been a substantial influence in my spiritual journey and professional growth. Louis, the opportunities that you have provided for me to explore personally, professionally, spiritually, and intellectually have been deeply rewarding and appreciated. Thank you for your friendship, your mentoring, your partnering on projects such as this one, and most of all for your time and patience. I am forever in your debt!

Foreword
By Thomas Moore

Every human life is full of challenges. We all have to make money to get along. We face the complexities of our childhood, our parents, school, bullies, difficult romances, sexual uncertainties, illness of all degrees and kinds, emotional volatility, aging, loss, tragedy and even the need to be creative and imaginative. It can be nerve-wracking just to be a person.

Our culture doesn't help much. We are living in a time when we think it's intelligent to consider the mysteries of human life as problems to solve. We make everything into a science and a technology, cutting away subtleties and layers of meaning and emotional nuances and spiritual implications. We'd like every problem to be solved by a pill or some sort of chemistry or machine. We even talk about ourselves in mechanical metaphors, saying, "I'm wired to be a social worker" or "the mind is a wonderful computer" or "my batteries are running down."

Messages from the various cultural media scream at us, insisting that we hold tight to the current mythology of human life in which medicine is charmed by "evidence-based" treatments and psychotherapy is short-term and based largely on quantified studies. We don't trust thought and imagination and believe that if neuroscience can give us a locale in the brain that explains our behavior, we can take our philosophy books to the dump.

A few years ago I was sitting in a cinema in England watching a film that tried to link quantum physics and spiritual teachings, a reverse of the trend to say that physical reactions are responsible for spiritual experiences. About one-third of the way through I walked out, noticing that a friend, a noted poet, got up at the same time and walked out with me. The soul guy and the gifted poet left behind a group of spiritual adventurers being charmed by the allure of materialistic science.

And so I feel at home writing a few words in support of a book that appreciates the role of poetry in deepening our reflections on life's quandaries and disturbances. I'd like every psychology major in the world to read the brilliant introduction that doesn't miss a step in keeping us close to our humanity and offering solid, profound and reliable ideas for navigating the complex ways of the most ordinary life.

As I read the poems, I had many different reactions: I felt stunned at new insights, I made notes, I memorized, I cried and thought of poems I might write, though I'm not what you'd call a gifted poet. This is therapeutic poetry, but I mean the word therapy in a special way. I always keep in mind Plato's idea that therapy is service, akin to caring for a horse, Socrates says. This is poetry that stands on its own but is especially useful when you are in one of life's dark nights or tunnels. It doesn't cheer you up; instead it takes you deep in thought to the mysteries working themselves out in what you feel to be problems and challenges.

All therapy, not just the professional kind, should be poetic. We could tell our life stories as profound fictions or mythologies giving us an undercurrent of meaning and purpose. We could turn to poets for insight or just for taking us down far enough in our reflection to glimpse the powerful narratives playing out below the surface of experience.

As I write, I'm in the midst of publishing my translation of the Gospels. I came across a line that stopped me and made me think. Jesus says, "I speak in parables." It's a simple line, and I wonder if he's saying, "Hey, I'm a poet. Don't misunderstand me. I like stories. Everything I say is poetic. Don't forget." So I translate the Gospels thinking all along that Jesus is a poet with a mission to raise the world up a step in its spiritual and psychological evolution. I think the authors of this book are also poets with a mission. They want to teach us how to reflect more deeply on the mysteries that stump us and move us emotionally and bring us to a pregnant point of fruitful wonder.

I've never been much of a purist. Some poets might not like linking poetry so directly to personal experience. I have no problem with it. When I taught at a university, I didn't feel comfortable with so many professors at ease in their ivory tower, not willing to step into the muck of ordinary life, to spread their knowledge in intelligible language and in ordinary settings. The sublime and the dirty keep each other honest.

Let me be the teacher and give you some instructions: Read the introduction carefully. Then read it again slowly, highlighting the words that strike you. Send the best ones to your friends. Start a conversation. Then read the poems in any order you like. Let your

Foreword

desire lead the way. Memorize a line or two or a full poem. If you're really engaged, drop a note to the poet or the editor. Then write a poem of your own. Be active in this reading. Read aloud at times. Try an old Japanese custom, and write a poem in response to the one you just read, sticking to the theme of the poem. Finally, live a poetic lifestyle. Get to the point where you can say of yourself: "I speak in parables."

Introduction:
Journeying into the Wounded Soul

> Let me keep distance, always, from those
>   Who think they have the answers.
> Let me keep company always with those who say
>   "Look!" and laugh in astonishment,
>   and bow their heads.
>   ~ Mary Oliver (2010), "Mysteries, yes"

There is a risk in writing about spiritual struggles. Spiritual struggle is often misperceived as confusion, resistance, a lack of faith, or spiritual weakness. A temptation in writing about spiritual struggles is to provide a clear path or an answer. The story of this book is very different. Instead of a definitive path, we are offering relationship, a shared community of those wrestling with the unknown in pursuit of something sacred. Instead of an answer, we are providing acceptance and voice in the dark night saying, "It is okay to be here." It is our belief that for many, spiritual struggle is not evidence of any problem but rather the heart of authentic spirituality.

If you are looking for answers, we do not provide them in this book. However, if you are looking for comfort and a community of fellow spiritual sojourners, we hope you find solace in the words of this book and, as a result, feel less alone. Although we do not provide answers, we hope that in these poems and the searching contained herein, you may find some direction.

The Lonely Walk

> There must be thousands of people
> in this city who are dying
> to welcome you into their small bolted rooms,
> to sit you down and tell you
> what has happened to their lives.
>   ~ Franz Wright (2006)

In the documentary *The Ties That Bind*, Bruce Springsteen discusses trying to build a community of sorts through the stories on his album, *The River* (Zimny, 2015). Each of the characters on *The River* is struggling with difficult realities of life. Within these struggles, existential loneliness appears over and over. Existential loneliness is different from just feeling lonely or alone; it is a type of loneliness rooted in our nature. While we can never fully overcome some forms of loneliness, through building a community of people struggling together we may feel less alone and the remaining loneliness may feel more manageable. One of the beauties of Springsteen's stories is that even though the particulars may be different from our lives, many people relate to the nature of the struggles being faced. There is a recognizable existential element in them.

In *Journey of the Wounded Soul*, we have similar hopes. Many who are facing spiritual struggles also face a deep existential loneliness. It is not easy to disclose one's spiritual struggles. Within many spiritual communities, it is taboo to share spiritual struggles or questioning. When they are disclosed, they are often greeted with superficial answers and clichés that send a message that these struggles are not okay. To find others who embrace this lonely walk and share in the experience of spiritual struggles can be a powerful. This connection helps individuals transcend the loneliness, even if for just a little while. In these connections, hope is found.

Idealizing Spirituality

> The very thought of becoming perfect or healthy or enlightened is riddled with ego. Why worry about the level of your progress when there is a world of people in need of whatever sensitivity you have?
> ~ Thomas Moore (2002, p. 115)

In contemporary culture, spirituality is often idealized. Someone finds God, or Buddhism, or mindfulness, and their life dramatically changes. All of a sudden, they are at peace and happy. We hear these stories and want to believe them. And maybe, sometimes, there is truth to them. Yet, for many people who experience these dramatic changes, they are short-lived followed by a gradual return to normalcy. Some changes may remain, but the more dramatic ones tend to fade away.

Many spiritual people believe that if they are not happy and at peace, then there is a problem with their spirituality. Even if they struggle inside, there is an intense pressure to act as if everything is all right. They work to keep the appearance of the change, but the feelings no longer match what is seen on the surface. Sometimes this pressure is coming from themselves; however, often it is from the implicit messages from their spiritual community.

The problem with idealized spirituality is not that it is false, but that it can be dangerous. When people have the belief that spirituality should solve all of their problems and that does not match their experience, it is easy to assume they are the problem. After all, it cannot be that there is something wrong with God or their spiritual tradition; it must be something wrong with them.

Idealized spirituality is often quite fragile. It does not have the depth to sustain individuals through difficult times. When everything must be just right for them to sustain their spiritual beliefs and connections, then they are bound to be disappointed. In reality, spirituality is quite messy... and that's okay. There is power in this messiness.

Doubt, Questioning, and Unknowing

The Tao that can be named is not the eternal Tao.
~ *Tao Te Ching*

The presence of God is more real to me now than it ever was, and yet it is also emptier of ideas and certainties.
~ Thomas Moore (2002, p. 127)

Doubting and questioning are two common forms of spiritual struggle and are the focus of many poems chosen within this book. Theologian Paul Tillich (1957), one of the great defenders of doubt, noted, "If doubt appears, it should not be considered as the negation of faith, but as an element which was always and will always be present in the act of faith" (p. 22). Similarly, Rollo May, an influential existential psychologist, noted, "The relationship between commitment and doubt is by no means an antagonistic one. Commitment is healthiest when it is not *without* doubt, but *in spite* of doubt" (May, 1975, p. 21).

It is often through the process of doubting, questioning, and wrestling with one's beliefs that they become real. When individuals simply accept what they are taught, the beliefs are often a shallow assertion of agreement. This belief is rooted more in the person of authority espousing the belief than in the content of what is being taught. At other times, belief is assented to because of fear, such as the fear of rejection by one's family, friends, or spirituality community, or the fear of hell or eternal suffering if one does not believe. Authentic faith or spiritual commitment, however, ought not to be rooted in fear.

When one's beliefs are questioned and wrestled with it becomes necessary to find one's own answer. This answer does not need to be found in isolation. Often, the questioning is done as part of a relationship or community; however, the final conclusion must be one's own. A community that accepts this process can be a powerful part of helping one find the answers that are being sought.

Finding one's own answer does not mean the ending of doubt; often, it means embracing the doubt and not knowing. Thomas Moore notes, "If any act is lacking sacred emptiness, it becomes full of itself and turns into its opposite, a defensive edifice against the cleansing power of mystery" (p. 11). Moore is using emptiness in the sense of not knowing, or recognizing that a deeper form of knowledge or wisdom is rooted in the recognition that there is something more beyond what we are able to comprehend or understand. There is a type of wisdom that can only be known in experience, because it is beyond what words can capture. There is a wisdom that is rooted in mystery and awe, and our ability to accept that we may never find *the* answer.

Yet, Moore (2002) also notes,

> When people feel the inadequacy of their knowledge, they may rush to fill in the gap with nervous belief and excessive information. Modern science and education are full of defensive, worried attempts to prove what can't be verified. (p. 12)

Schneider similarly states,

> Our greatest challenge today is to couple conviction with doubt. By conviction, I mean some pragmatically developed faith, trust, or centeredness; and by doubt I mean openness to the ongoing changeability, mystery, and fallibility of conviction. (Schneider, 1999, p. 7)

Danger is rooted in the denial of doubt and limitations in our ability to know, not in doubt itself. In this, we can recognize that our ability to come to grips with our doubt and accept them as a spiritual gift or blessing.

Dark Nights of the Soul

> We need suffering in order to see the path.
> ~ Thich Nhat Hanh (1998)

The concept of the "dark night of the soul" emerged in the Judeo-Christian tradition from the writing of St. John of the Cross. However, this concept is often misunderstood and has relevance for other faith traditions. It is common for "dark nights" to be used to refer to any time of suffering by a religious person; however, this is not what St. John of the Cross was speaking of.

For St. John of the Cross, "dark nights" referred to a period of transition in one's spiritual beliefs where many of the previous structures and rituals of faith no longer provided the same meaning. It was not a loss of faith or spiritual beliefs, though many experiencing dark nights worry that they are falling away from their beliefs. Rather, it is a transformation emerging from a spiritual struggle.

James Fowler (1981), who wrote about stages of faith, spoke to a similar period of transition. Fowler interviewed many people from different faith traditions to develop his theory of faith development. The fourth stage was a reflective period, which for many is experienced as a spiritual desert or moratorium. This as a period of questioning, but for Fowler it is also a period of transition and growth. It is an expected part of the development.

In the dark nights, many people transition from concrete spiritual symbols to focusing on what the symbols represent. Instead of emphasizing specific traditions, they seek the meaning that the traditions represent. Instead of focusing on concrete rules and laws, they try to understand the underlying meaning of the rules and laws. It is not surprising then that many who have experienced these dark nights become more accepting and tolerant of others and of differences in belief. This tolerance and acceptance does not mean that they are any less committed to their own spiritual convictions; it reflects a greater openness to others and the spiritual paths that others follow.

Dark nights are one of many forms of spiritual questioning, and not everyone experiences these in the same way. Furthermore, it is somewhat of a misnomer to speak of the dark nights as a stage, which would suggest it is confined to a period of time. Aspects of the dark night are ever-present for many people who engage in spiritual struggles. The dark nights represent a more concentrated period of struggle and transition. Yet, relevant to the focus of this book, many approaches to understanding spiritual development reveal that there is typically a period of intensive questioning, doubting, and struggling that represents a part of the spiritual journey. When these are avoided, spiritual growth can be limited.

One illustration of how the dark nights can be illustrated is in the poem, "An Empty Soul." In this poem, Fehl states,

> If God cries, does he experience my pain?
> If God sees, does she recognize my anguish?
> If God speaks, does he know I am lost?
> If God is, is she aware I am also?

In this deep and honest questioning, the essence of what many experience as the dark night can be seen. There is a loss, a present emptiness revealed. As the poem concludes, however, we see suggestions of hope:

> When my life is limp and hopeless, keep the glory within my sight.
> When my heart is aching and its beat is fading, keep the light burning and help me focus on its flame.

While in the midst of the dark night, we see that there is still a faith or a spirituality connecting to something deeper.

Finding Community

> ...hope cannot be said to exist, nor can it be said to not exist. It is just like the roads across the earth. For actually the earth had no roads to begin with, but when many men pass one way, a road is made.
> ~ Lu Xun (1921/1959)

People who engage in spiritual wrestling often find community in surprising places. As therapists and educators, we have found clients and students who have had powerful awakenings upon realizing they had more in common with people from different spiritual or religious traditions who engaged in spiritual wrestling than individuals from within their own tradition who did not. While there were obvious differences in beliefs, they found more comfort and community with those who embraced a similar path of struggle regardless of faith tradition. This can be one of the many blessings emerging from authentic engagement with our spiritual struggles—the discovery of a new and powerful community.

Relationships and community are important. Yet, community oftentimes limits potential growth by containment that prevents individuals from exploring their potential and alternative ways of viewing spirituality. While it is often healthy for community to provide some boundaries and security, these elements can become problematic when they are repressive and overly constraining.

Parenting provides a parallel example. Parents provide boundaries for children intended to keep them safe. However, for the healthy development of a child, the boundaries should be such that they also allow for freedom and exploration. As healthy children develop security in their relationships with parents, they begin to explore the world. At first, they will frequently check back with their parents to make sure they are safe and going in an okay direction. Gradually, parents loosen the boundaries and allow their children to explore. Through this process, children become more comfortable doing things independently. If they do not feel secure in the relationship with parents, they become too afraid to explore.

Some parents, fearful of their children's exploration, will not allow them to explore. They present the world as a scary place. This reinforces a dependency upon the parents rooted in deep fears and insecurity. While this may keep children safe in the short term, this fear on the part of the parents has negative psychological effects on children and does not prepare them for the confidence they will need when they can no longer remain dependent upon their parents for safety.

Spiritual communities can similarly provide safety for people to do spiritual exploration or questioning. When a spiritual community provides unconditional acceptance and is willing to support individuals in their spiritual journey, they are able to engage in a healthy spiritual growth process. However, when the spiritual community presents the world and any alternatives to their worldview as dangerous, the result is fear of spiritual questioning and exploration. Spiritual beliefs can become rooted in fear and insecurity, not in true authenticity. At times, this can lead fearful individuals to outright reject the spiritual tradition altogether.

Finding a spiritual community that supports individuals in their spiritual journey is essential for healthy spiritual growth and exploration. For some, spiritual questioning and wrestling is an ongoing part of their spiritual journey, while for others it may just be a point in time along their spiritual path. Regardless, a supportive community is important.

Spiritual Wrestling as a Spiritual Gift

As noted in the previous section, for some people the questioning can be a spiritual gift. The poem, "Waiting for a Blessing," is an example. Although the end of the poem is suggestive of a weariness of "waiting for the blessing," the poem itself reflects the paradox of the spiritual wrestling. Toward the middle of the poem, the poet states,

> I wrestle you between the light
> because it is the only way
> I know
> to hold You close.

This illustrates the paradox that a certain intimacy exists in the midst of the wrestling. In part, this is why we frequently use "wrestling" as a metaphor in this introduction to the book.

In Western society, we often compartmentalize our experience instead of revering its complexity. We separate suffering from joy, pain from happiness, anxiety from security, questioning from knowledge. Yet, in each of these cases, the seemingly opposite ideas are intimately connected if not necessarily so. Questioning does not mean that there is not concurrent knowledge, belief, and security. When we recognize that these co-exist, our experience of the spiritual struggle or questioning begins to change. We are able to be comfortable in the midst of the unknowing.

Wrestling with our Inner Demons

> I'm frightened by the devil,
> and I'm drawn to those ones that ain't afraid.
> ~ Joni Mitchell, "A Case of You"

> The heroes and leaders toward peace in our time will be those men and women who have the courage to plunge into the darkness at the bottom of the personal and corporate psyche and face the enemy within.
> ~ Sam Keen (1991)

> ...less and less is life animated through personal discovery, intimacy with others, or self-reflection. While life has become more manageable for many people, it has become commensurately less engaged.
> ~ Kirk Schneider (2004, p. 20)

Not only do we compartmentalize our experience, but our society also places a high value on labeling experiences as good or bad. Suffering is bad; joy is good. Sadness is bad; happiness is good. This dichotomous outlook often places a heavy load of guilt on the individual who struggles to engage with the feelings and emotions of both sides. In my own (Steve) experience, I grew up in an environment in which each experience and the associated emotions were labeled as good or bad, and most often emotions were labeled as bad. The outcome of this training has been a constant struggle with simply accepting my emotions and feelings for what they are instead of labeling these responses as good or bad, positive or negative. Most often this has meant stifling my emotional responses and holding back in expressing what I am feeling at any given moment in time. In addition, I frequently question my perceptions, as well as my instincts, about life and the choices and directions that are available for me to take.

Since the age of enlightenment more than 150 years ago, Western religions, in particular, have been caught up in a battle of factualizing beliefs that, up until the middle of the 19th century, had been accepted as matters of faith or as mystery to be embraced. The emphasis on fact and empirical evidence has brought about a much more rigid perspective concerning individual spiritual struggles.

In this context, individuals who choose to engage with questions concerning their spirituality do so with little or no support, and often experience antagonism for asking questions or making certain choices. People who courageously embrace the spiritual questions and doubts with which they wrestle are frequently judged as making a poor, if not a bad, choice.

This spiritual wrestling is not just limited to the question of the existence of a divine being, or what happens after death, or the authority of sacred writings. This wrestling often leads individuals to question the power and purpose of religious structures, practices, and doctrines. It is a shaking of their spiritual foundations, taking them beyond what they first envisioned when beginning their spiritual trek.

It is in this milieu of unknowns that one begins to reconstruct a spirituality that creates or renews a sense of purpose for one's life, as well as a new worldview or perception of relating to that which is greater than oneself. As the poems in this volume suggest, this is a struggle not undertaken by the faint of heart. It is a wrestling that forces one to face his or her darker side, to name and confront those demons that have dogged him or her for years, maybe even decades. In this struggle, the individual is challenged to overcome the demons within or to acknowledge their presence and develop mechanisms that help cope with their presence. Wrestling with one's spirituality is to learn to live in and with many shades of grey, recognizing there are few, if any, absolutes by which he or she may live his or her life.

People use spirituality in different ways. At times, spirituality ends up being used as a defense against fears and anxieties or for some egocentric purpose. This may lead to using spiritual beliefs to justify judgments and condemnations of other groups of people or to justify words and behaviors that cause harm to self or others.

However, spirituality can also provide the security to allow for us to be more honest about our own inner demons. It should be noted here that we are not using "demons" in the sense of some external entity or reality that possesses or influences us. Rather, we are using "demons" in the sense of what Rollo May (1969) refers to as the daimonic. For May, the daimonic was something natural that was part of all of us, and holds the potential to be used for good or ill. He also notes that it carries with it the potential to overtake one's personality, thereby becoming destructive. A couple of examples may help clarify.

People have a natural urge to want to feel good about themselves and to feel valued. This, in itself, can be very healthy and help one to develop positive self-esteem or self-confidence. However, this confidence, if over-developed, can also overtake us in the form of narcissism, excessive self-promotion, or self-centeredness. Similarly, people have a normal sex drive, which serves to support healthy intimate relationships and procreation. However, some people become overtaken with their desire for sex. When this occurs, it is self-destructive and can also lead to destructive sexual behaviors that harm others. May (1969) maintains that when one represses or denies these "daimonic" potentials, they can grow more powerful and have the potential to over-take the person's better judgment. To prevent this process, May advocates for finding ways to integrate these potentials into who we are and use them for creative purposes.

May, who wrote extensively about creativity and the arts (see May 1975, 1985, 1991), said that these daimonic potentials could be channeled for creative use. In this process there was redemptive power through art, including poetry. Throughout this volume, we can see examples of this creative process. In the poem, "Be Still," by Michael Moats, there is a rather explicit internal conversation of struggle. Though different judgments and justifications are considered, the end of the poem provides the answer: "Love/Love/Love." Though it may sound cliché, love is the answer.

Poetry and the arts can also provide a vehicle for self-exploration, including getting in touch with our inner demons and our deep wounds. May (1985) states,

> Good art wounds as well as delights. It must, because our defenses against truth are wound so tightly around us. But as art chips away at our defenses, it also opens us to healing potentials that transcend intellectual games and ego-preserving strategies. (p. 172)

Similarly, Gradilla (2015) states that, "in all ancient societies poetry was seen as the purest and most dangerous form of truth and knowledge" (p. 7). In these quotes, we witness the beautiful paradox of poetry and the arts, particularly as connected to the healing process. The arts can open us to new awareness of ourselves and the world. These insights can be beautiful, but they can also be painful, even devastating, at times. Poetry and the arts, however, hold incredible power to create meaning and provide healing despite the pain.

When we trust that there is something more, or feel compelled to face the darkness in search of something more, then the arts and our spiritual struggles become powerful allies in this pursuit of growth.

The Danger and Possibility
in Contemporary Religion and Spirituality

Obviously, all religions fall far short of their own ideals...
~ Ernest Becker (1973, p. 204)

The Destructive Potential of Religion and Spirituality

Although we have focused mostly on spirituality thus far, it is important to give some attention to religion as well. Our religious and spiritual traditions and institutions are not what they used to be, particularly in the United States. It seems that we have altered their purpose from seeking the sacred and transforming ourselves to simple pop psychology. On Sunday morning, from many pulpits preachers translate pop psychology or offer simplistic theologies of happiness. Mindfulness and meditation have been co-opted and changed into ways to overcome our anxieties and other psychological difficulties. Our religious and spiritual rituals either bore us or lead to detachment, particularly as we no longer recognize what they are pointing toward.

Worse yet, too often religion and spirituality are used to justify our hate, anger, and violence. We blame those who hold different beliefs for the evil in the world, all the while using our own beliefs to deny and justify our own harmful acts and intentions. Still others use religion for marketing or in the service of seeking greater power and influence over others.

It is no wonder that so many have lost faith in our religious and spiritual traditions! Yet, it is not our intention to denigrate religion or spirituality. Just as all people fall short of their ideals, all religious and spiritual groups and institutions, which are comprised of fallible human beings, also fall far short of their ideals. Just as we do not reject all people based on their imperfections, we should not reject all religious and spiritual traditions based upon their imperfections.

In contemporary culture, religion receives harsher criticism than spirituality, which is often idealized. Or, as H. Newton Malony (2005) noted, "Spirituality is in; Religion is out! So goes popular culture" (p. xv). Historically, religion and spirituality were not separated as frequently as they are today. As the conception of religion and spirituality has evolved over time, religion has tended to get much of the "bad stuff," while spirituality keeps the "good stuff" (Hoffman, Hoffman, Hoffman, & Cleare-Hoffman, 2010). The corruption, such as has opportunistic televangelists who have swindled people out of money or engaged in inappropriate sexual exploits, is given to religion, while personal meaning and freedom is given to spirituality. This separation is unfair to our religious traditions.

Hoffman et al. (2010) note that this separation has been needed for some to be able to retain some connection to the sacred. In other words, the disgust at the corruption of religion has provided a barrier for some in their pursuit of the sacred. Through separating religion and spirituality, they have been able to retain the connection to the sacred.

This anger at religion is reflected in the poem, "Collecting Christian Sentiments." Over the years, I (Louis) have read this poem publicly many times with many different reactions, including strong reactions in very different directions. The intent of this poem was not to be anti-religion, or anti-Christianity. In a paradoxical way, it was an attempt to retain a connection to the religious tradition I grew up with in the midst of so much that I found problematic and distasteful. The poem was successful in this endeavor.

While the separation of spirituality and religion discussed earlier has helped salvage a connection to the sacred for some, it does so with some costs. A more honest appraisal of religion and spirituality recognizes that religion and spirituality will always be limited as understood by people. Even if the essence of religious and spiritual experience is perfect, we can only grasp or relate to it in our limited human form. We can never experience religion and spirituality in their purity, thus we will always distort them to some degree.

While it is evident that much harm has been done in the name of religion, it is equally true that much good has been done in the name of religion. We should not use the good to justify the bad, nor should we use the bad to discount the good. At the heart of all the major religions of the world is love, compassion, and concern for others. The destructive use of religion should be attributed to people claiming the religion, not to the religion itself.

If we are to save religion and spirituality, we must be willing to be honest about them, critique them, and wrestle with them. Furthermore, we must be willing to accept the limitations of religion as conceived, understood, and practiced by fallible human beings. According to Tillich (1957), the root of idolatry is treating human-made symbols and interpretations of the sacred as being ultimate truth. Religious and spiritual symbols, traditions, and even beliefs are intended to point us toward the truth, but they should not be mistaken for the truth that is beyond what we can grasp or comprehend.

Authentic spirituality, as well as authentic religiosity, is about seeking the answers, not finding them. It is rooted in a humility of belief or faith that recognizes that the answers are beyond us. Thomas Moore (2015) conceptualizes religion stating, "In my in-depth understanding of the word, religion is our creative and concrete response to the mysteries that permeate our lives" (p. 2). This is a refreshing take on religion in a world that often distorts its meaning and is quite different from the typical definitions of religion.

Religion and spirituality often become dangerous when it is believed that they provide *the* answers. This is why the renowned existential psychologist, Kirk Schneider (2004, 2009), focuses on the concept of "awe." For Schneider, awe embraces a sense of mystery and appreciation for something that is beyond oneself; beyond one's ability to grasp. Appreciation for the unknowable and mystery is what Schneider believes to be an essential component to alleviating many of the problems of our contemporary world. It may also be essential in alleviating the problems in our religious and spiritual traditions.

Valuing Religion and Spirituality
Engaging our spiritual struggles, doubts, and questions is a powerful way of valuing religion and spirituality. Spiritual struggles and doubts should not be viewed as a lack of faith, belief, or commitment, but rather as evidence of all three.

As we noted before, as definitions of religion and spirituality have evolved over time, religion has been associated with the structured, communal, and organized aspects of our pursuit of the sacred. These purposes have often been devalued. Yet, it is essential that we recognize their value in a non-defensive way. Religious institutions have accomplished good and they have caused harm. Throughout history, religious institutions have cared for the suffering and those rejected by the community. Religious institutions have been a pillar of advocacy for human rights, such as in the civil rights movement. Many religious institutions have been advocates for peace and the humane treatment of all people. Religious institutions also provide hope, comfort, and community for many people. Just as no individuals would want to be judged on their sins alone, we should not judge religious and spiritual institutions and traditions based solely on their mistakes and limitations.

Many people in contemporary society have found it easier to be spiritual, even religious, outside of organized religion. For others, without the connection to the religious and spiritual institutions, there is something important missing from their lives. It is important that we honor both of these paths in the pursuit of the sacred.

Spiritual Struggles in Sacred Texts

Buddhas and bodhisattvas suffer, too. The difference between them and us is that they know how to transform their suffering into joy and compassion.
~ Thich Nhat Hanh (1998)

When I applied my mind to know wisdom, and to see the business that is done on earth, how one's eyes see sleep neither day nor night, then I saw all the work of God, that no one can find out what is happening under the sun. However much they may toil in seeking, they will not find it out; even though those who are wise claim to know, they cannot find it out.
~ Ecclesiastes 8:16-17

And about three o'clock Jesus cried out with a loud voice, "Eli Eli lema sabachthani? That is, "My God, My God, why have you forsaken me?
~ Matthew 27:46

Having been raised in a conservative Christian church, I (Louis) found comfort in an unusual piece of scripture. Although my spiritual wrestling began in high school, it really became more prominent for me while attending a conservative Christian college. I often received the message from friends and professors not to question. At times, this was explicit; however, more frequently it was implicit.

It was in this context that I began finding great comfort in the words attributed to Jesus, "My God, My God, why have you forsaken me?" If Jesus could say these words, if it was okay for Jesus to ask such a bold question, surely it was okay for me to do so as well. This became one of my favorite pieces of scripture, and maybe the one that influenced me the most. When I was told—explicitly or implicitly—"you can't ask that!", I found comfort in these words.

I was fortunate, too, to have a theology professor, Paul Vasconcellos, who was a powerful model as well. I remember sitting in his systematic theology class, which he taught with lectures that were quite passionate, and a question about doubting arose from a student driven to tears of fright by her questions. The student asked, 'How do I know if I really believe with all these doubts?' Dr. Vasconcellos, who lectured with great energy and passion, suddenly changed. His entire presence was different, having transformed to an embodiment of compassion. He said, 'If you are worried about your doubts, then you believe.' Since this time, I have journeyed far in my spiritual beliefs, but I know the permission found in this scripture and in Dr. Vasconcellos's teaching, were powerful for me in developing a more authentic spirituality—one that embraced frequent spiritual wrestling.

The sacred texts of various world religions are filled with stories and poems of spiritual struggles. Indeed, some of the most famous poetry ever written can be found in the sacred texts, often embodying spiritual struggle. Over and over in the scriptures of the world religions, the words promise struggling and suffering along with hope. Yet, in contemporary culture, we often focus solely on what appears clear or mostly clear while discounting the very prevalent themes of mystery and awe. What is unclear is also often distorted into the appearance of clarity. If we read the sacred scriptures of the world religions honestly, we see clear embracement of spiritual struggles.

Being with People Experiencing Spiritual Struggles

People experiencing spiritual struggles with increasing frequency are seeking out counselors and psychotherapists instead of their religious/spiritual leaders or community. This, in itself, is quite telling. For many, the resources within their spiritual tradition for dealing with spiritual struggles do not feel safe. Those who question and struggle fear judgment and condemnation. However, the bigger resistance is often rooted in the superficial answers and clichés they receive. They may be told things such as, "This, too, shall pass," "Just have faith," or "Let it go."

Our society seems to have lost its capacity to be with those who are suffering. We are quick to judge, label, or diagnose people who are experiencing suffering, and we have relegated suffering to something that should be dealt with by medication, mental health professionals, or other specialists. We no longer take care of our own, but rather castigate them.

In Bruce Springsteen's (2012) song "We Take Care of Our Own," he sings of examples in our country where we have not taken care of our own, then laments,

> Where're the eyes, the eyes with the will to see
> Where're the hearts that run over with mercy
> Where's the love that has not forsaken me
> Where's the work that'll set my hands, my soul free
> Where's the spirit to reign over me
> Where's the promise, from sea to shining sea
> Where's the promise, from sea to shining sea
> Where's the promise, from sea to shining sea
> Wherever this flag is flown
> Wherever this flag is flown
> We take care of our own
> We take care of our own

We live this lament every day. As therapists, it is evident that there would be much less of a need for our profession if more people knew how to be with others who are suffering. Instead, it seems evident that the need for mental health professionals is destined to continue to grow as we more and more don't take care of our own—our own family, our own friends, our neighbors.

People with spiritual struggles do not need answers but rather acceptance, relationship, and hope. Individuals not comfortable with spiritual struggles may inadvertently encourage spiritual stagnation. If spiritual struggles are part of a growth process for many, then the quick solutions provided by others and discouragement of staying with the spiritual struggle can hinder or block spiritual growth.

Many professionals also struggle with this. If we have not done our own spiritual depth work, and if we have not found a way to be with our own spiritual struggles, it is difficult to be with the struggles of others. This is not to say that we need to have experienced and resolved all our own spiritual struggles. For many, this never happens. In fact, people who continue to wrestle with their spirituality are often more comforting and helpful to those in the midst of a difficult spiritual struggle than those who seem to have reached a state of certitude.

In supervising therapists in training over the years, I (Louis) frequently have found that trainees as well as other professionals with strong spiritual beliefs struggle more in helping people encountering spiritual struggles than those who may not identify themselves as religious or spiritual persons. There are many reasons for this; however, some similarities also are evident. For instance, it is common for therapists to feel the need to defend God or the religious tradition. Others feel pressured to offer answers, even if they are comfortable not providing answers to other issues that arise in therapy.

For this reason, when devoutly religious and spiritual people are seeking a therapist or counselor, I often do not encourage them to find a religious counselor, such as a "Buddhist therapist" or "Christian therapist." Instead, I encourage them to find a therapist that works with religious and spiritual issues from various perspectives and will honor their beliefs. It is less important to have a shared belief system than it is to have a therapist who will respect and support your beliefs and allow you to do your own exploration.

In the end, the qualities that prepare someone to be effective with others experiencing spiritual struggles are compassion, empathy, and an ability to be with the unknown. With these qualities we can be present with someone without the need to rescue them or provide them with our answers.

Isolation and Engagement

When the emphasis in spirituality is placed on it being personal and individualized, it is easy for spirituality to become isolated, ego-centric, and self-centered to varying degrees. Spirituality needs community, too. As we have noted, this is part of our hope with this book—to create a sort of community for people who are wrestling with their spirituality.

When spirituality is focused on the individual and one's own spiritual progression or attainment, it is often disconnected from engagement with the world. In response to this, some scholars, such as Donald Rothberg (2006), have advocated for *socially engaged spirituality*. An important, but often overlooked, aspect of spirituality is ethics, which points beyond the self. From the perspective of socially engaged spirituality, an essential part of our spiritual growth is preparation for responsible and ethical engagement in the world.

Our spirituality is not just for our own personal well-being, but a foundation for helping others.

Ethics, in this sense, should be distinguished from following moral laws. In contemporary culture, it is common for ethics to be reduced to following rules. However, this is a very shallow understanding of ethics. Similarly, ethics should be distinguished from being a disciplined person and being able to follow a specified spiritual regimen. Instead, we are using ethics in the sense of being engaged in the world in a loving, compassionate, and caring manner. This may look different in different spiritual traditions, but the heart of an ethical approach is concern for others.

Spiritual struggles can sensitize us to the struggles of others. It is hard to develop compassion without suffering. While it is important not to idealize suffering or suggest that we should seek it out, it is important for us to recognize the gift that suffering can bring. To be very clear, we are not suggesting that tragedies or intentional harm by others that lead to suffering are good or justified by the gifts of suffering, but rather that when we open ourselves to the unavoidable suffering that exists in the world and our lives, we can be transformed by it in positive ways. In particular, this can help us become more compassionate to others who suffer.

Henri Nouwen (1972), in his book *The Wounded Healer*, sees our openness to our own suffering as an important aspect of our ability to be with others in a healing capacity. Similarly, Marc Barasch, in his book *Field Notes on the Compassionate Life: A Search for the Soul of Kindness*, recognizes that self-compassion serves as an important basis for being compassionate to others. Being compassionate towards oneself is an important concept in the Buddhist tradition; however, the purpose of self-compassion is not simply to be self-serving. Rather, it is to help develop a capacity for compassion for all people.

Individuals who are resistant to acknowledging their own wounds and suffering often are not very effective at being compassionate or empathetic with others. As a professor training people in the field of psychology, I (Louis) have noticed that there is often a resistance on the part of therapists to acknowledging that they, too, have struggled with problems in their own life. *This is ridiculous!* It is as if admitting that one has suffered disqualifies one from being a therapist. If anything, the opposite should be true. I will often state to students, "I would hate to see a therapist who has never tasted suffering themselves." The intent with this is to prompt students into thinking about this differently.

The same is true with spirituality. I would hate to have a religious or spiritual leader or counselor who has never acknowledged their own spiritual struggles. Suffering is universal, and all spiritual people experience spiritual struggles. Denying or repressing these does not qualify us to be counselors, therapists, spiritual guides, or religious leaders. If anything, it should disqualify us. Our own wounds and spiritual struggles are an essential part of our preparation to be healers.

Patience and Timing

The art of working with spiritual struggles—our own and those of others—is finding the appropriate timing. In spiritual development, if we are thrown into questioning too soon, it may result in the lack of belief instead of growth. The avoidance of spiritual struggles can lead to rigidity or fear-based spiritualty. Yet, all of these are possibilities and not an exact formula. *Our* spiritual paths are just that: *our individual spiritual paths*. When sitting with others in the midst of spiritual wrestling, we cannot assume that their path will be the same as ours. Thus, the art is to be patient with ourselves, and patient with those with whom we are walking on their spiritual journeys. This is why the best guides are those who walk along side, simply reflecting, observing, and accepting. Directions too often just get in the way.

The only way for us to get the timing right is to be patient. We cannot force the questions. And we cannot force the answers. We cannot pursue the dark night but must let it pursue us. If we seek suffering it will be hard for us to find the meaning in suffering once we have discovered it. If we remain patient and open, the timing will reveal itself.

The final poem in this book, "When a Student is Ready," reflects many of the themes discussed in the introduction. A little girl asks an innocent and beautiful question to Agnew, the author of the poem: "Are you an angel?" His response was silent reflection. But her mother, out of her own discomfort, responds:

> She was patient, staying attentive
> even when mother
> wrapped arms
> around shoulder

> pulling her in saying, "Ah honey... no."
>
> Attempting to sooth
> embarrassment
> that was not there.
>
> A teaching of play it safe
> masqueraded as,
> being loving,
> molding
> conditioned,
> limited, closed minded
> thinking into place.

The mother's response was a simple, innocent gesture with good intentions. Yet, it held back the innocent curiosity, hopefully without discouraging such questions for the future. Maybe if we stayed open to these innocent questions of youth, then spirituality in our world today would be freed to flourish. But alas, we tend to shrink away.

This poem also speaks to timing. Agnew heard the the little girl's question at a time in which he, as an adult, could hear it as a lesson and reflect upon it. The poem closes with a sentiment that we hope readers of the book, too, will leave with after reading the poems within:

> The young girl so beautiful.
> Thank you.
> I know myself better.

The Approach of *Journey of the Wounded Soul*

> Dogmatism of all kinds—scientific, economic, moral, as well as political—are threatened by the creative form of the artist. This is necessarily and inevitably so. We cannot escape our anxiety over the fact that the artists together with creative persons of all sorts, are the possible destroyer of our nicely ordered systems.
> ~ Rollo May (1975, p. 76)

Our hope in this book is to help people to embrace their spiritual struggles and perhaps feel less alone in doing so. As the quote from

Rollo May above illustrates, creativity is a powerful force in helping people to break through their resistances and rigidities to experience a deeper level of freedom. While this freedom can be scary, as it challenges our "nicely ordered systems" and beliefs, there is a more powerful and authentic meaning to be discovered on the other side.

As we started to collect poems for *Journey of the Wounded Soul,* we were intentional to include a wide range of poets and poetry from various spiritual traditions. Our preference was for poems that were accessible. There is a difference in poetry that is written purely for the intention of art versus poetry written for healing and growth, although the paths frequently intersect. Poetry written for healing and growth emerges from an authentic emotional space and seeks to engage it. This may be true of poetry written for the sake of art as well. However, with poetry written for healing and growth there is more primacy given to ways that poetry serves these processes as opposed to focusing on the artistic qualities. Thus, there are differences in the types of poetry included in this volume as compared to those found in a typical poetry book. While we believe all the poetry in this book to be good poetry, and many of the poems good enough for literary journals, our review of poems focused more on the ability of the poems to reflect engagement with spiritual struggles.

We hope this book can be transformative in various ways including deepening your understanding of spiritual struggles, encouraging you in your own questions and struggles through the poetry, and inspiring you to write your own poetry on spiritual struggles. If you do write your own poems, we encourage you to focus first on your own healing and growth process. This needs to be primary. Many people are afraid to write poetry out of fear that it will not be good. Yet, much like the avoidance of spiritual struggles because of fear limiting our spiritual growth, avoiding writing poetry for fear it will not be aesthetically pleasing limits our spiritual, psychological, and artistic growth. The purpose of writing poems about spiritual struggles is not to impress literary critics, but rather to inspire your own soul toward healing and growth.

Including a wide range of poems was also intentional beyond the aesthetics. Individuals are drawn to different types of poetry and poetic expression. Most who read this book will not be drawn to every poem in the book. It is rare that we read any poetry book, even by the great poets, and are enthralled by every poem. We hope that in the diversity you will find poems that speak to you and poems that draw you to return to them over and over again for further reflection. We also hope the diversity of styles will inspire you to try writing different types of poetry. At times, a style of poetry that may not be your favorite as you read may still be powerful for you when writing poetry yourself. In other words, we hope the diversity of poems included will encourage freedom in your own poetry explorations.

In concluding, this has been a powerful book for us to compile and, in many ways, we have felt connections with the various poets who have contributed to this volume. While we know some of the poets, we have never met the vast majority of contributors to this volume. We only know them through the poetry and our brief exchanges around the poems. Yet, we sense connection, even community, beginning to emerge through the poems. We hope, as you read these poems, you will begin to experience this community as well.

References

Fowler, J. W. (1981). *The stages of faith: The psychology of human development and the quest for meaning.* San Francisco, CA: Harper San Francisco.

Gradilla, A. J. (2015). Foreword. In L. Hoffman & N. Granger, Jr. (Eds.), *Stay awhile: Poetic narratives on multiculturalism and diversity* (pp. 7-8). Colorado Springs, CO: University Professors Press.

Hanh, T. N. (1998). *The heart of Buddha's teaching: Transforming suffering into peace, joy, and liberation.* New York, NY: Broadway Books.

Hoffman, L., Hoffman, J. L., Hoffman, J. L. S., & Cleare-Hoffman, H. P. (2010). Culture, religion, and spirituality: How spirituality saved religion. In J. H. Ellens (Ed.), *The healing power of spirituality: How faith helps humans thrive* (Vol. 2: Religion; pp. 191-206). Westport, CT: Praeger.

Keen, S. (1991). The enemy maker. In C. Zweig & J. Abrams (Eds.), *Meeting the shadow: The hidden power of the dark side of human nature* (pp. 197-202). New York, NY: Tarcher/Putnam.

Zimny, T. (Producer & Director). (2015). *The ties that bind: The river collection* [Motion picture]. United States:

Lu Xun (1959). My old home. In Y. Xianyi & G. Yang (Eds. & Trans.), Lu Xun: Selected works (Vol. 1; pp. 90-101). Beijing, China. (Original work published in 1921)

Malony, H. N. (2005). Introduction. In R. H. Cox, B. Ervin-Cox, & L. Hoffman (Eds.). *Spirituality and psychological health* (pp. xv-xviii). Colorado Springs, CO: Colorado School of Professional Psychology Press.

May, R. (1969). *Love and will.* New York, NY: Delta.

May, R. (1975). *The courage to create.* New York, NY: Norton & Company.

May, R. (1985). *My quest for beauty.* Dallas, TX: Saybrook.

May, R. (1991). *The cry for myth.* New York, NY: Delta.
Moore, T. (2002). *The soul's religion: Cultivating a profoundly spiritual way of life.* New York, NY: HarperCollins.
Moore, T. (2015). *A religion of one's own: A guide to creating a personal spirituality in a secular world.* New York, NY: Gotham Books.
Oliver, M. (2010). *Evidence.* Boston, MA: Beacon Press.
Rothberg, D. (2006). *The engaged spiritual life: A Buddhist approach to transforming ourselves and the world.* Boston, MA: Beacon.
Schneider, K. J. (1999). *The paradoxical self: Toward an understanding of our contradictory nature.* Amherst, NY: Humanity Books.
Schneider, K. J. (2004). *Rediscovery of awe: Splendor, mystery, and the fluid center of life.* St. Paul, MN: Paragon House.
Schneider, K. J. (2009). *Awakening to awe: Personal stories of profound transformation.* New York, NY: Jason Aronson.
Tillich, P. (1957). *The dynamics of faith.* New York, NY: Harper & Row.
Wright, F. (2006). *God's silence: Poems by Franz Wright.* New York, NY: Alfred A. Knopf.

Poems

Waiting for the Blessing

Louis Hoffman

For Johnny, with gratitude

god
we've wrestled
for many years.
I feel your
weariness growing

you know
my fight
is sincere
I don't challenge you
for enjoyment,
or ego,
or even the pure pleasure
of rebellion.
I struggle
because it is who I am;
I struggle
because it is the only way
for me
to Be.

I wrestle you between the light
because it is the only way
I know
to hold You close.

many years ago
in a dark night
a friend shared the familiar story
of the night you spent
with Jacob
wrestling through the darkness

waiting for the light
Jacob—a mere mortal—
would not be overtaken
and you blessed him

and so here I am god
wrestling in the dark
waiting for your blessing
I feel you close
like never before
and I will not let you go.
but when, dear god,
will you give your blessing?

Always Sunset
Steve Fehl

It is always sunset in my world . . .
. . . always sunset.
Never dawn, nor noonday sun . . .
. . . but always sunset.

As the sunset turns to dusk,
. . . I am captured by these mountain fortress walls,
     which hide the light and tease the dawn.
And in this place my life unfolds –
. . . imprisoned by the shadows hold.

Sunset is never early, nor ever late,
     in suits of blacks and grays ashen images come to life,
     and mingle with faceless figures overcome by strife.
As light fades and dusk emerges,
the shadows grow,
and all becomes a drab mosaic of never darkness and never light

This is the world in which I live . . . the never dark, but never light
Doubt, discouragement, fear, and pain,
hopelessness, helplessness, failure, and distain,
incompetence, isolation, rejection, and despair
accompany me everywhere . . .
. . . in this place of never dark, but never light

It is always sunset in my world.
Every morning filled with grief, each evening bringing no relief.
The masks I wear hide so well,
the ache that dwells within me here . . .
. . . in this world of never dark, but never light

It is always sunset in my world,
a place filled with lifeless swirls.
No God to brighten up my path,
No savior to rescue me from the Sacred's wrath,
Only shadows in this cold dark place
Where faceless bodies congregate.

This is my world ... of never dark, but never light.
And so I wonder ...
... what might be for me, in this canyon of no glee
How might I move beyond these walls ...
... to smell the birth of a morning dawn ...
... or feel the light of the noonday sun?

Passeggiata with Saint Francis
Lorraine Mangione

We walk
You hold my hand
lead me through
the dark passages
down the stairs.
You always went first.
The light above,
the frescoes by Giotto,
the earthquake fissures
the glory of God,
the bright light of
transcendence the colors
Giotto dared to use
They dazzle us
but we cannot stay there.

You let me look and visit
but we must go down
into the cool into the dark
not so close as the catecombe
no the air is more sweet here,
the space is bigger,
the sanctification is immense.
San Francesco is immense
is a traveler of the world,
of heaven and earth
and many places in between,
is here, in my heart, always,
and now you, are here, also,
in this darkness, walking with him
in his visions, in his death,
walking with you—airy but powerful,
no substance but all substance,
filling me up, filling up the spaces.
Why did you leave?

And how is it you are here?
In the crypt, in the grave,

as I circle the grave of this
greatest Saint,
Saint of Sun and Moon,
San Francesco
A spirit strong enough to hold
your strong spirit.
I didn't know you would be here,
but how could I, now,
have ever not known?
The path has been so muddled
without you. Where did you go,
sister, navigating off on a tangent,
now the paths come clearer,
come as one, once again—Complete!
In this realm of dark, of cool,
of eternal moment.

Coal Town Hospice
Robert A. Neimeyer

On the banks of the Ohio,
far from the namable places,
the town squats, wounded.
The sturdy girders
of the bridges carry cars
away, away,
across the brown expanse of river
bleeding these hills,
across the tracks of the C&X coursing
with their loads of coke
and steel. In the pre-dawn drizzle
Main Street stands empty
as the stores, their vacant eyes
leaking the dreams
of grandfathers.

On either end of town tower
the Goliaths of the plant, the refinery.
They announce the descent
into this valley, bar the exit,
squelch hope with belching fumes.
Between them the town crouches,
subservient.

There is still work here,
deposits to be made
to bank accounts,
      to lungs.
The cancer sends its metastases
winding down the wide streets,
the back alleys.
The eager tendrils find the unstopped
cracks under doors, the open
windows, mouths. For the young,
there is one sure way
out.

It is here that hospice
does its dark work,
lays its light hand
on laboring chests.
The plants have set down roots
in the furrowed brows,
sewn seeds of need
in the fertile flesh. Questions seep
like oil from the pores.

Like history,
nurses have no answers to give.
They fill the beds, fill the bags
hanging on steel poles,
coax the anodyne
into collapsing veins.
With each loss, chaplains
suture the wounds with familiar verse,
lay the dead to rest in the scarred soil.
Social workers apply their gentle press
to the bereaved, nudge them back to life,

back to the factories. In the end,
the survivors carry the memory
on their bent shoulders,
feel the heavy hand of obligation
that follows them to the furnaces,
to their homes,

like grief.

Manufracture
Richard Bargdill

God, god? oh my god!
Don't talk to me about god.
If god lived he lived
in the hungry hunter before the kill.
If god lived he lived
in the rain during the drought.
If god lived he lived
in the death after the plague.
If god lived he lived
in screams of a man running into bad odds.

Odds too killed god!
Pascal turn god into a gamble
and each of us into a bookie.
Place your bet
pick your mysticism.
We may no longer be able to
understand Aristotle,
and we may no longer know god.

He does not live in the rain
we have irrigation!
He does not live in hunger
we have mickey dees!
He does not live in the scream of the soldier
We drop our bombs from screens!
He does not live in our things
We make so many things.

You can make me new fruits to feed me.
You can make me new cloths to clothe me.
You can make me new drugs to heal me.
You can make me new bombs to protect me, but
Can you make me a god?

A Simple Game with Stones
Sean Gunning

Through the blinds
I see a host of sparrows on a gravel path
overgrown with crabgrass, weeds, and sand,
bumping breasts like doughy boys from the suburbs
before tip-off in a fat camp basketball game
they'd rather not be playing in
on a sunny, Sunday afternoon.

I watch them reverently —
as cheery African children not yet teens —
playing a simple game with stones
against the wall of a small and spartan home
on a bone-dry day
a continent away;
a lifetime away;
a few feet away.

I didn't give much to Live Aid
all those years ago,
or even watch the concerts on TV or DVD,
and on Sundays, with the host on my tongue,
I pass the frailest, eldest eyes
in the foremost pews,
whose bodies bend,
whose breasts beat,
whose souls believe
they will one day
flutter, sigh, and soar towards the highest tree;
and in their eyes, I see me.

And I think about
all the children all around the world,
who are hungry and sick and crying and dying,
and I hope enough is being done
by other people —
all those wonderful people —
to feed and care for
the millions of children

who one day might want to play,
might have the strength to play,
a simple game with stones
with other children
from around the way.

A Little Sesshin to Soothe My Soul
Virginia (Gina) Subia Belton

~~why zen now? he asked~~
hurts. it hurts. it hurts.
how to stop this suffering?
gaze into its eyes.

~~no religion~~
self. no self. cushion.
what is this "devotion" for?
to hold open heart.

~~the right action of no action~~
we struggle to stay
upright and elegant, yes?
and now my back hurts.

~~sitting is nothing special~~
soft front. straight back. sit,
silent, still and awake.
commonplace cushion.

i breathe so softly
into the weary heart of
soul and suffering.

~~Zen dog~~
i bow to "Chika".
you are the soft and furry
Bodhisattva here.

~~black robes in the wind~~
clean path to Dharma.
no proselytizing here.
standing still he smiles.

Leaves
Glenn Graves

Aspen will fall soon
Birch and Maple will follow
All become Gold first

Preparing For My Medicine Dance
Candice Hershman

The insides of my arms are smarting,
as if tiny beaks are pecking hard at my skin shell,
wanting to sprout wings so I
can fly out a bird dance.

If I spin fast enough,
maybe I could catch air,
matching my childhood dreams
in which I could fly
over all that daunted me.

If I crouch low enough to the ground,
maybe I could gather dust,
warm as the underbelly of a snake
that knows nothing else but
to press itself against the earth
and be close to all that beckons me.

If I arch my back enough,
letting my head lift to the sun,
neck paradoxically alpha exposed,
arms stretched out with open palms
and hard spread fingers of no grasp,
heart completely agape
in a refusal to close after hurt,
asserting like the vestal virgin of a ship,
strutting forward in defiance,
maintaining a personal territory of love
that is only about being . . .

Maybe my medicine for myself
can become medicine for the world.

Drawing an Angel
Carol Barrett

Begin as God began:
with breathing.
Float the shadow
of despair.
Float more and more.
When the image floats
off the easel, answer
the back door.

***

"Drawing An Angel" was originally published in the book *Drawing Lessons* by Carol Barrett (Finishing Line Press, 2002). Reprinted with permission.

A Very Thin Line
Paul T. P. Wong

A very thin line
Of invisible ink
Beyond which
There's no return

The farthest reaches
Of the human mind
Cannot comprehend
What lies behind
The darkly shroud

Death was kind to her
A much needed rest
After a long rough ride
No fears no regrets
Just looking back
With a kindly eye
She waved goodbye
With a gentle smile

Now descending alone
Into the bowel
Of dark cold earth
Sealed by a rock

Over the vast expanse
Of time and space
I hear the echoes
Of Calvary Hill
On this day of Passion
A double death-blow

But the earth can't defy
What heaven declares
Nor can the grave
Hold back
The seed of life

Here we all stand
On snowy ground
The world of tombs
Bear silent witness
To lives lived and
Deaths mourned

Beside her resting place
A lone birch tree
Tells its silent tales
Of falling leaves
Weeping in the wind
But whispers to my ears
The return of spring

Wandering through
The fantasy land
Of gracious living
Desperately seeking
A golden moment

Then by chance
I stumble upon
The face of tomorrow
Just beyond
The setting sun

"Potter to the Pot about the Wheel" (Isaiah 29:16)
Ted Mallory

Be still

virtues are not instantaneous

some gifts
only come
through suffering

The Struggle
Nathaniel Granger, Jr.

Tired,
Broken,
So broke,
Can't pray.
I simply come home
And go to bed.

False Prophets
Nesreen (Alsoraimi) Frost

Here she comes again
That soft and broken girl
That hard and open girl
That nature driven
Simple and complex soul
Who can see logic dancing
Around more solid truths
The pull is strong
With all the muscle of emotion
With every primal magnetism
Pragmatism
Gone
As I let her take over
My reasons fly high
I shoot them in the sky
Feathers float
Remnants that are meant to carry guilt
I'm so intoxicated
I don't notice them lying
All around me
We complicate
We stratify
We complicate
We rectify
What was meant to bend
And expand
Wide and narrow
Layered
And messy

You can't possibly see so clear

That was the greatest cue
False prophets
With plastic expressions
Binary and institutionalized
How can you be so sure?
I can trust those with some doubt

And humility
Always guessing and assessing
It's all we can do
Embrace uncertainty
Open to understanding
Or risk living with eyes closed
Or risk living in ego
Pride
Belonging
Superiority
I won't let it rule over me
Let them decide who I will or will not be
Won't censor my words
Or my curves
Basic and unchanging truth prevails
Love
And more love
Nature is love
And love is our truest nature
I can't dress it up any other way
To make her look less naive
More mysterious or challenging
No, she is in my soul
In your face
Everyday
Simplest of answers
Simplest of commands
Simplest of deities

Ode To A Teenage Life
Steve Fehl

Her ponytail bobs up and down in the air,
    As she glides down the floor like a fawn with no cares.

Her expression is intense,
    No hint of awareness of the crowds screaming presence.

Her hair is bright red and her eyes deep green,
    A reminder she was born on the day of green beer with corned beef and hash.

The sounds of the ball thumping on the floor surface,
    Shoes screeching and squeaking;
    Are sounds that give comfort and solace, if only for a while.

These sixty minutes on a hard wooden floor,
    Bring relief and some respite,
    From a family life of confusion, of crisis, and pain . . .
      sometimes even more.

The circles and borders of the oak colored floor provide shelter
    From the yelling, the hitting, the put downs she too often
      experiences
    In the place she calls home.

The referee's whistle,
    Her teammates hand slaps and hugs
    Give her life clarity and direction she only dreams of at home.

Her ponytail bobs up and down in the air,
    As she glides down the floor like a fawn with no cares . . .

A Feral Innocence
LeesaMaree Bleicher

A tempered skin
Sun soaked memories
Where once… I hopped… too
Rain drenched realities
You wonder why I stay?
I am right where… *I am supposed to be*
One step forward… two steps back…three steps to the side
A dance that leaves me breathless
For that matter… there is beauty in the chaos
Peace in the pandemonium

I buried a bunny today…in all his feral innocence
I saw my own rage raw and untamed
As the dirt sifted through my fingers
Falling upon the snowy white fabric of his bones
It spelled it all out so clearly
You belong to… *all of this* and my story… if I tell it
Will be my freedom
So… will yours

Not Even Tinsel
Lorraine Mangione

Such a dark, dark time.
Such a time when the lights
from the tree could not shine
past the ends of the branches,
and the sparseness could not be
hidden by silver threads of glitter.
A time when Christ was made
of glass, and lay unsung in
a far corner of the room.
Not a single wassail could
lift the dirging chorus that
captured all in its grave-tones.
Even a smile was no beacon
to run toward in such gloom.
And there is no telling where lies
the top when no light infuses;
And there is no telling where
a hand and a door could meet,
or if there is a hand or a door.
Quite a time, when night
lowered in early, every night,
to claim the world from
the sparkle of day.

Something in Those Blue Eyes
Louis Hoffman

For Amaya

there was always
Something
in those
peering blue eyes
Something wise,
silently observing
Something insightful
I often heard people say
you could see right through
to their soul
and they were afraid
but not me
there was just
Something
Something wild
Something beyond

they'd scoff
when I said
you were part of my
Spirituality
but there was Something
in those
blue eyes
where I saw God
felt God
knew God
Something that showed
the wildness of
nature
the vastness of this
universe
not Something to be
controlled
understood

tamed
there was just Something

now that you're
gone
I struggle
to find God
it's not that you're gone
but that you're
not here
not with me
not showing me
I can't find the way
anymore
but keep trying
remembering that Something
in those
blue eyes
you'd want that
you cared when I was sad
and liked when I found peace.
in those blue eyes
I could see that

Yet
there's still Something
in those
blue eyes
no longer
with me

Colorado to New Hampshire
Lorraine Mangione

The last time I was above tree-line
a young boy died
a boy just old enough to begin to be
called a man
a boy of lank and height but inscribed
within an angel's shawl.
Because we dared to trek through spaces
of alien planetscape
in the sere-bright light of air so far
from how people live
and thrust ourselves above boulder and cairn
to hail the sun
the sky opened up and plucked him from
the bleating land.
This time it is a Japanese cragged dome
of fog and cliff–
angles of black and gray slice in hexagons
at each other
while moss drips, rocks drip, pine hugs
the ground and drips;
Mist hides in silk shreddings a notch
in the bluffs
where water slides across a path and all
is slipping downward;
Curtains part wispingly as I
tremble in descent
but redressing is swift and I glance
back to nothing.

Visitor!
From where hail ye?
And to where dost though journey?
Only for a moment
Only by the grace of some
      mirthless spirit
          are we allowed to pass.

Not even an old monk hermit
    on these peaks–
Look to the path
    for that is all you have.
Nay, there is no path.

Blessed End; Sorrowful Beginning
Rodger E. Broomé

His son's death was a blessing.
Standing there solemnly surveying the costly medical equipment,
Tubing, tape, wrappers; Toys were among them
He was 10 years old and struggled each day.

Love, devotion, duty, sympathy, and many other motives sustained the man; Providing for and preserving his son; Faithful perseverance.
Doctors, insurance, medication, with no hope that his son would ever play ball, kiss a girl or even do an honest day's work for an honest day's pay.
Today was unknown, yet expected – Perhaps even silently prayed for its hastening.
Dad called mom and told her that *it* was Today.

Make a soft yet stable place.
Manage the order of affairs.
Document, communicate, and console.
For Today was a Blessed end, yet a sorrowful new beginning for this family.

Life now has a lot more space and free-time will be uneasily welcomed.
Missing the boy will provide more space without the medical equipment...and toys.
More free-time without the frequent and long drives to doctors, hospitals...and the zoo.
Relief comes from the absence of crying, labored breathing...and giggles.
Dad talks of his son playing in a Better Place now. Eternal reunification, maybe?
The home is a better space, but not a better place, for mom, sister...and dad.
What a beautiful Sunday morning...Today

His son's death was a blessing...

End of Report

Inevitability
Tamiko Lemberger-Truelove

Every second we come closer to death
The finitude of life lingers in the wide smiles of youth who so foolishly seek after their own undoing, eager for time to begin, grieved by its steady pace, incredulous at its seeming lack of urgency

But those of us who are standing on the precipice of existence simply pray for uninterrupted delays
That the winds will steal the slippers from time's feet before it pilfers more of our fragile lives away from us.
We pray for more time, more of everything, not less.

Last Christmas
Hajnalka Kurti Woosley

It was the day before Christmas, my favorite of all.
The phone rang in the distance – I knew it was *that* call.
The answer came so softly from my feeble mouth -
I wanted to scream, I wanted to get out
Of this Universe of hypocrisy,
Man-made, fake Christianity!
I wished to run away.

His voice was soft, only I would sense that he was crying.
He shared the vexatious news then waited trying
Not to sob. If there was a god he surely
Hated us.

My finest friend, my epitome, one who always has been
There when need arose in my existence's frail spin.
She was a paragon between the fallen rust -
Glowing with tenderness, amity and trust.
"She was" – as grandpa delivered those words
We both began to weep in strains,
And wished to run away.

We would roam this forsaken Earth, scramble from North to South
Looking for vindication, begging with lusty shout
For answers. If there was a god he surely
Hated us.

We would search from East to West, in order to find ointment
To heal our sorrow, abomination and torment.
We then would seek revenge like Attila the Hun
For past, present. Laugh with no fear just fun
In the face of the future. Feel pity
For our deranged society
Wishing to run away.

Together in that moment we commemorated all she was
And swore the oath that no human abstractions, no flaws,
No law or destiny will ever erase Grandma's sweet memory!
As grandpa and I were willing to devote our eternity

Cherishing her while trying times may sway,
No longer wishing to run away.
Craving to stand and keep the flame
Of love diffused in her name.
If there was a god
Reigning in Zion
Or Abaddon
We prayed he
Grant her
Rest.

Panning
Robert A. Neimeyer

    ~for Alex

Since the diagnosis
I have been panning for gold.

Alone in this river, I brace
against the onrush—
inexorable, consistent,
pulling me downstream
with its cold hand.
For now, I find a foothold
in the stony bed.

My limbs stiffen, numb
in the chill current,
the pain in my gut
        forgotten.
The rush of water muffles
the voices from the shore,
the common industry of towns.

The same flood that presses me away
frees the glistening lumps
laced through the matrix upstream,
tumbles them seaward.
Waist high in foam,
I bend, plunge, delve
the sturdy pan into the scree,
draw up the find.

With practiced eye I spy
the glint of a vaster orb above,
a silent witness,

and turn my face to god.

                ***

This poem was written as a spontaneous response to a friend whose email announced the recurrence of an adolescent cancer, now Stage 3-4. The insights that have followed, he said, felt like gold panned from a cold stream. I closed my eyes, typed the poem in a fluid whole, then edited for typos and polishing.

Silent Night
Jyl Anais Ion

It was a day of waiting
and a spot
a touch of blood
shed,
letting go of what was no longer
needed.

I waited for you
and there was nothing but silence.
Today, my body fell silent, too
my womb empty
with nothing more to let go of.
I wonder what evoked this night.

Water table
expanse of embryonic
fluid that makes the earth inhabitable
the floor where I sit
and create, from

the womb that is emptying
into another stage
and the release I want to feel with you
like the swell of rising tides

my womb,
the holy grail.

The End of Self
Tamiko Lemberger-Truelove

Days have become quiescent
The hour has grown loud
The minutes are not satisfied without
Confession.

The flesh has been
Flayed, down to the crust and bone of spirit
While self is devoured by divinity
Abjuration is lighter than truth, though each
Stride from providence is cemented in pain

There is no point to this
Nothing will shelter me from you

I acknowledge your name because
There is no other choice

Though it is immutable that I
Shall suffer, while seeking you

Filing A Soul Exemption
Candice Hershman

I misplaced my soul,
somewhere in this pile of bills,
the ruckus of street demolition,
city permit fees and home ownership,
student loans for free thinking,
interest rates high,
wages low to average,
the blunder of bureaucracy
that despite unfairness,
I always have to pay for
with the little time I have left,
proving my credit to those who can't be trusted.
Everyday there is a form to fill out,
and even if it would only take minutes,
the cumulative effect is like chinese water torture,
a drop a day on my forehead for all time,
slowly driving me either mad
or into a haze of consumptive addiction.
I count each tedious mark.
Dealing with numbers makes me feel like one.
I don't want to be a number.
No, I am not a number.

My marrow is an army of rebels
pushing up hard against the ceiling of my bones,
marching towards spontaneous combustion,
that photo of Quang Duc after he lit himself on fire,
famous monk, did it matter?
I had to look up your name,
but please know,
I haven't forgotten how you made me feel.
The futility is just another match
tossed on an internal pyre of hopes,
the dreamsmoke choking out the living,
surviving aspirations crawling out on all fours,
looking to get away from
the ouroboros inferno,
ring around the rosy,

child's games not child's games,
but a firey death dance
of rage:
domestic despair.
I understand why some people decide
to no longer care,
but I am a poet
and have come to realize,
I am kin to a long line of revolutionaries.
Even when I write my joy,
I am filing an exemption
from the taxes that are off the record.
With each poem,
I am trying to be born.
This is my howl.
This is my affliction,
yet soothe to my scorn.

The cat rests.
I envy him.
I wonder if I have him
to keep something wild close to me.
He pays no bills or taxes,
is accountable to no callers.
He waves his tail like a playful mast.
along with his sister feline,
lies on God's green earth,
not once feeling deprived of a bed.
There is no question.
Not even of his soul.

And me?
I am tied to the clock,
drawn and quartered by angst and exhaustion.
Thanatos screams.
I want to burn it all down.
Then, I would mock the ashes.
Nakedness in the midst of nothingness
sounds off natural reason
as I long to shed my skin.
I want to live simply

so I may simply live.
My favorite cliché
that feels strangely uncommon.
I want no accountability
except to those I love
and those who wave a flag of virtue.
That is my longing,
and so I continue to investigate,
to file a soul exemption,
a sacred resurrection,
so I can live again.

Animal & Angel
David Bentata

This is the fable
which Aesop has not told
about two very different *creations*
together part of the *foundations*
of yet another universe bold

Forced to live as one
for as long as the cycle is lasting
the Animal wanting its *pleasure*
while the Angel its spiritual values will *treasure*
in one same body bound.... yet contrasting

Of such differences is Man created
His Animal side needs pleasures
Food, sleep, sex, all part of its *role*
base hungers that need full *control*
and must be given in the right measures

But Creation has balance built in
His Angel side also has its desire
to improve from just being all *beast*
wasting precious time in eternal *feast*
from pleasures which will never inspire

So... much as the Animal alone
is noble in its natural state
it cannot rise above its fixed *self*
created to remain static on its *shelf*
to live and die and in between that, find its mate

But the Angel inside us all
is the only free agent of Creation
with choices from which to *choose*
whether to win and improve.... or to *lose*
and if lost it will require reincarnation

To return for yet a new cycle
and learn once again the full reason

for having been returned to this *jungle*
learn to walk straight & narrow, not *bungle*
and master its Animal side without treason

Such is really the balance required
of us all in this physical life
to be Master and not the *enslaved*
from our Animal partner be *saved*
and so.. free our Soul from this recycled strife

The Human Legacy
Monir Saleh

The prime culture of humanity
Knows neither east or west
Nor any class or race.
Put aside the man-made fences;
Let your soul transcend in grace
All horizons, even the rainbow's trace,
That we may be the Almighty's welcomed guests
    Where there is no more" you" and "I".

Boundaries are for the divided lands
But you're invited to a higher place,
To an impartial ground;
Where you will merge into that flock of doves
Deep in the timeless blue sky
And fly towards the eternal supremacy,
Our hands clung tight together where
No power can sever them apart.
And we will sing the song of peace, and unity, and love
Beneath the serene shade of the global olive branch
Within that golden light, that's not so far away,
    Where there is no more "you" and "I".

Everywhere is east,
For our terrestrial world is round
And the sun glows warmly on us all.
Forget about the time and place.
A melody may mirror such a grace.
Beyond the darkest of the night
The dawn will soon arise
With glory in the sky.

But be aware!
    The essence of all happening is only there
        Where there is no more "you" and "I".

In Praise of Sheep
B. M. Lyon

Even as I slip from the lap of Buddha
I recall the Ten Commandments in Technicolor
verses of the Koran on the internet
the Sermon on the Mount.
Though never a Catholic
when all else fails I recite a Hail Mary.
Pilgrims crawl the Camino de Santiago de Compostela
or lie prostrate under stars
fixed in their placement long before
the stone mason built this broken cathedral.

Commandments, confessions, forgiveness, love
we need them all to quiet the demons of self
the fears of the other keeping us apart, on guard
punctuating the headlines of our dreams.
But must we have Crusades? Inquisitions?
Witch trials? Jihad?
Must you believe what I believe?

Perhaps we know too little believe too much
lamentations for Galileo who knew too much
believed too little.
How much easier to be a shepherd of sheep
who fears only the wolf and sleeps well
after counting his flock

or better yet, to be the sheep.

No Samaritan
Sean Gunning

I went down Wardlow to Woodruff yesterday
and saw a man lying on his side on the sidewalk,
his torso in a bird of paradise landscaped verge
between Ralphs parking lot and the sidewalk,
and the man and the landscape almost blended
into suburban invisibility.

"There was a man who went down
from Jerusalem to Jericho, and bandits
attacked him and robbed him and beat him
and left him with little life remaining in him,
and they went away."

At his side, I passed through the pungent death-cloud.
Not a physical or spiritual death,
but a death of determination
to keep striving;
beaten down;
born into desolation;
and I recognized the smell of the grace of God.

"And it chanced a priest was going down that road
and he saw him and passed on."

I prayed to our father, the father of us both:
I'm no better man than he, just more blessed.
Fortunate to be married, to have a home,
to have the worries and the unfulfilled dreams that I do.
I'm no better man than he, just more blessed.
And I knew that was not enough.
And I passed on
not wanting to be late for an appointment.

"And likewise a Levite came and arrived at that place
and saw him and passed on."

I prayed to our mother, the mother of us both.
And I reclined in the contoured dentist's chair,
thinking it poetic that the man resembled Doctor Roe,
with his black hair and black beard
and grey and black clothes,
and I resolved to look more closely
if he was still there on my way back.

"But a Samaritan as he journeyed came where he was
and when he saw him he had compassion on him.
And he came to him and bound up his wounds
and poured on them wine and oil,
and he put him on his own ass
and brought him to the inn and took care of him.
And in the morning, he took out two pennies
and gave them to the innkeeper
and said to him, take care of him,
and whatever you spend more,
when I return I will give it to you."

And he *was* still there.
Now lying north-south
with his arms straight at his sides
and his feet crossed — thick grey socks
with a gaping hole at the ankle.
And his face was ashen-brown or olive-colored
or a shade of white or black.
And his beard was scraggly and tangled and filthy,
and sorely lacking
the dark, designer dashes of Doctor Roe.
And he was lying on Woodruff Boulevard
at 1:30 in the afternoon, with closed eyes
inside a grimy-grey hoodie shroud,
listening to the faint sound
from the other side of the street
of the L.A. River
carrying discarded debris back to sea,
and the faint footsteps of the people passing by.
And I passed by,
and prayed for him a second time;
knowing it was not enough;

knowing I was no Samaritan.

***

Previously published in *Cadence Collective*. Reprinted with permission.

Grant Me A Second Chance, Lord
Paul T. P. Wong

I cannot break through the stone wall of silence
Nor can I bridge the gulf of misunderstandings.
There is nothing I can do to repair the damage,
No amount of apologies can make up for the hurt.
Please grant me a second chance, Lord,
To start anew and make things right.

I have messed up my life real bad,
And I have been to hell and back.
Eating bitterness as my daily bread
And washing my face with tears each night,
I've paid the price for all my wrongs,
And You have paid my debit with death.

Will You hear my desperate cry?
Will You lift me from the horrible pit and
Set my feet on higher ground?
There is no turning back the clock,
There is no undoing of what I've done.
Will You grant me a second chance, Lord?

Redemption
David N. Elkins

I don't care if you've made mistakes in life
I don't care if you've been a liar, cheater, or thief
I don't care if you've been in prison
I don't even care if you once betrayed someone you loved

I want to know if your human failings have made you humble
If they've made you more tolerant and loving toward others
who, like you, also carry the weight of past sins

I want to know if you can acknowledge your sins
without making excuses
If you can confess your betrayals
without expecting to be forgiven
If you can shoulder the burden of your own biography
And trudge slowly and faithfully to a place where, at last, you will
Bless the chains of guilt
Praise the fires of remorse
Give sacrament to the albatross that forever shall hang around your neck
And bear, without complaint, the crosses on which you once crucified yourself and others

If you can do these things, redemption waits
You and I might be saved yet

The Human Condition
Emily Lasinsky

Love.
Created out of dust and love,
A spare rib for the second born-needed supplement.
Knower of all, yet couldn't predict this
fall.

Loss of lovers.
Given specific instruction,
    tempted-gave in.
First display of destruction,
First symbol of being human,
The beloved rejecting   being loved.
Didn't she know she was breaking Your heart?

Realized exposure-naked,
Beauty turned to shame.
Can no longer depend on the ground to be the source,
New Life requires pain.
Generations who have followed
can't believe it-can't believe that this is Love,
too hard to swallow,
too afraid to swallow anything.
Fear of repercussions
for moving to the beat of their own drums.

You wanted love.
We, I, broke your heart.
Striving to win back love-no need for strife.
Daily practice, but still hungry.
Just when I think my pallet is satisfied,
tragedy leaves a bitter taste,
emptiness doesn't go down easy.

Yet You expect me to press on,
Dig deep to my core, my roots,
Believing there's a purpose in this mission
    there's beauty in this pain.
Love...The Human Condition.

Starving Children
Wade Agnew

18,000 children
will die
from starvation today.

don't write about yourself,
God can't you think
of anything
more important?

But the other day...

when I brought food home,
and the neighbor's
children
asked
if
they
could have some

I backed up, growling at them.

***

Originally published in the book *A Desultory Way* by Wade Agnew.
Reprinted with permission.

Preacher Man
Louis Hoffman

Preacher man
Stands on the corner
"Repent and be saved!"
"You are all sinners in need of a Savior!"
I walk by
Eyes averted in discomfort

At a nearby coffee shop
Sipping $5 lattes with a friend
We talk about how religion
Has become corrupt
Our conversation turns
To politics then corporate greed
Sitting in harsh judgment
Calling out to no one in particular
"Repent!"

I remember my friend, Gideon
A soft-natured man
Who seemed unable to be judgmental
He spoke of being a street preacher
Standing on the corner
Calling people to Jesus
I knew if he said "Repent!"
It was from love
In the distance granted by many years
I finally receive his witness to me

Walking back to my car
Still uncomfortable
I smile and nod,
Preacher man still shouting in anger

That night
Listening to the political speak
I again think of Gideon
Breathe
And let compassion do its work

Falling for Fall
Kristen Beau Howard

The aspens drip with death
Who is it that sees?
My child in you, everything will change
It already is, don't you see
My child, please rest.
You see those aspen leaves? These right here?
The branches once held in green,
But now are brown
And shall be bare in freedom soon
My child, please rest.
Please rest like the aspen trees.

Nature's Refuge
Larry Graber

Once again
I'm saved by
My hills

So good to see
them rolling
And calm,

expansive
Against
my cringing
torso

Fresh from
Motor reminders
Disgust & Shame
Feeling dirty

The not-to-be-seen
Silenced
Sent to their rooms

They wreak
havoc below words

In my body
refreshed sequences
truth's language
implicit Forms
The layers of my youth

Pain and body tension
Disgusting food
forced upon me

I stuff it down

Emotional expressions
on Dad's Face

Both parents'
looks of lost control

Anxious Sister
Damaged

People wanting
to hurt
one another
& doing it

Enslaved dilemmas
EnForced control
Mini freedoms
Exert toll

Never any comfort
For the scared child
Living in fear

Forced elsewhere
to seek refuge
In nature

Or to check out
Disconnect from feelings
Retreat into intellect
Or disconnect, period.

Seeking comfort
only led to Words,
and to Questions

No hugs,
No somatic relief

Occasionally,
there were

eventual looks
of compassion
from Mom

These (had to) sustain me
As my body and insides
Shrunk and disappeared

On my hills now
I am safe

I hear giggling
In the distance

A fond relief
to my ears

My body relaxes

I am here
Now

I see
ocean's gleam
The sounds of birds
Hikers in conversation

Sitting on this rock

Again and Again
I return to
the world

As my body
remembers
I record
its words

recovery
is eminent

In the sanctity
Of nature's womb
Alive & Connected
Whole & Complete

Blessed
by Nature's Refuge
I am home

Autumn
Steve Fehl

It is autumn
and the light fades
darkness comes too soon
Beige, brown, purple, red, gold, and rust
The wind chills, the rain is cold, the snow is wet
The ground is hard
Life is gone, and
the world goes quiet

It is autumn
My soul is dark and
my heart is cold
Hope is lost and a dream forsaken
Loneliness chills, isolation grips
I struggle again
Life is empty, and
my world is quiet

It is autumn
Heart-ache rules
It holds me until I acknowledge its embrace
Confusion rides upon a headless horse . . .
no direction is clear, no purpose emerges
Red, black, blue, purple, gray
The dark night holds sway as I seek the light

It is autumn
My life and my world have grown silent
as I seek love, warmth, trust, touch, and embrace
As I seek a God beyond winter.

Saint Fido
Dan Hocoy

I don't pray anymore.
Since I stopped keeping score.
Of the times I felt deceived.
And was just told to believe.

Why all of this suffering and pain?
I know...the original human stain.
But it's hard for my mind to conceive.
That all of this came from Eve.

Does my yearning suggest a diety?
Or merely a lack of maturity?
I don't need true verification.
Just a little communication.

Revelation is uncommon they say:
"You should look for signs in the everyday;
God appears in the leaves and morning fog".

I guess...at times...
I do see the Divine.
In my dog.

Medicine Woman
Juanita Ratner

Powerful medicine of love
Bathed in alertness
Wanting never to miss an opportunity
To warm a soul
To life

Relentless friendliness
Expressed as healing spirit
Radiating through her friends
Concern gives sight
Of blocks within or doubts

And with the chisel of her words,
Now sharp,
Now reassuring
She sculpts for them
The figure
Of their deepest thoughts

Courage born of love
Through mothering
And mentoring
And learning to stand firm

Now grounded as a tree
Her heart extends like branches
She listens
And the sound of anguish
Stirs her being
Like leaves rustling in the Wind

Her strength to care
Nurtured
In the matrix of the Spirit
Where she rests in silent depths
The Source of her being
And all that binds us
Into One.

Simpler Times
(A Cantankerous Old Man's Perspective)
Nathaniel Granger, Jr.

Without thought
bowels moved.
Reflections,
directions,
erections achieved
without thought.

One pill.
Without thought,
a Flintstone vitamin.
Thirteen now,
red and yellow
and pink and green

Without thought
all for this,
a blue one for that.
Yes, that.
For God's sake
Why is the damn lid so tight?!

A Path?
Tom Greening

I'm glad I'm not a frightened refugee
swept from my home by heartless history
to wander on rough seas to some strange place
with feeble hope of guidance from God's grace.
Too many drowned, but some are still afloat
adrift in life on some half rotten boat.
That child, born in a manger long ago,
is he someone who can lost migrants show
a path to safety from disaster and
a better life in some new promised land?

Idea of Reference
Hans Cox

Eternity in death is long,
Life short. Do not fear,
With trembles, the sidewalk sirens' song,
Unreal thoughts' immurement of your mind,
Untoward blinks from one whom you pass near,
The change of your step as you leave him behind.
Still these things bother me. I can't belong;
But so long lost when found remains long lost.
There is no telling when your shadow crossed
Mine, nor who you were among the stoking throng,
Nor what our missing meeting cost.

Checkmates and Exes
Nesreen (Alsoraimi) Frost

Unstable mixes
Casting hexes
Creating murals
Of funeral processions
I haven't learned my lesson
Obsession and possession
Session after session
I fraction off pieces of me
Some intact
Some covered in messy
Debris
Facts get muddied
Particles get studied
Body and mind
Soul full of ideals
And empty
Appeals
Surreal and high speed
You're leading me
You're leading me
Astray
Facing tears
Facing fears
Separating from
Phrases
That had me under a spell

This nomadic dwelling
Keeps me wandering
Quenches my
Thirsty heart

I camped for a night
Stomped my stakes
Into the ground
Until
The magic was fading
And I started paying

More attention
Until my heart felt empty
And my reasons were plenty
For fleeing the scene
Packing my vagrant dreams
And catching a ride
On the wings of
Stranger thoughts

The absence of danger
Filling up
Drilling spots
For more bolts
Holding my bones
Together by the hinges
Contingency plans
Include:
Taking the pieces apart
And dislocating the joints
Wringing out
My heavy heart
Filling each lung
With equal parts
Of smoke
And air
Laughter and despair
Those always make
A lovely pair
Blank stares
Will follow
Emotions will get swallowed
And digested
Suggestions
Beat down and arrested
For lack of reason
Inconvenient timing
For this type of
Injury
This type of melodramatic
Tragedy

Day by Day
Sean Gunning

With hope, with love, like-formed from molded clay,
you ask for me to be a better man.
It draws me in, but then you push away.

And with the sun, your smile returns each day
to ask for more than just an average man.
It draws me in, but then you push away.

And when I'm down, you tell me don't dismay;
you ask for me to be a better man.
You say you're there with me along the way.

But I don't always feel it when you say,
"You can do it, son. I just know you can."
It draws me in, but then you push away.

You grant free will to choose to sin or stray.
You ask for me to be a better man.
To keep the faith, and yet be kept at bay.

This game that you have made so hard to play:
you ask for me to be a better man;
I try to learn the rules, I kneel and pray.
It draws me in, but then you push away.

On Hadrian's Wall
B. M. Lyon

With our fingers we trace the lichen
descended from lichen that etched these stones
when first chiseled by a Roman soldier.
Between the meadows of Britain and highland crags
he stood his watch in drizzle and sleet
torn sandal strap whipping in the wind.
From this wall he guarded fields with muddy paths
tracked by innocuous sheep.
Did he miss his homeland? Not Rome
but some conquered village in Gaul
where he was wrenched from his father's dead hand.
Sheltered, clothed, and fed
with fellow conscripts former hunters and farmers
a seduction more effective than brute force
each harboring a memory of home
isolated by his own mother tongue.

Somewhere in our DNA persists a magnet
that draws us ever homeward
like a river in reverse
we recede in time and space
till we are all in the Garden of Eden
of our recollection.
And when we are there naked
before fig leaves and scars
will we finally recognize
ourselves in each other?

First Religion
David Bentata

There is a country at war...
A war costing *millions*...
a war against another
not just other lands.......but brother against brother!
A war killing both soldiers and *civilians*

There is a country at war...
Not just one, sadly there are *many*
who incited by faith and creed
(or slogans fed by their puppeteers greed)
pay with lives valued at merely a *penny*

The riches gained by the victor
basking in his blood-paid *opulence*
it has to be said
he will lose it when dead
needing his spiritual penance to *cleanse*

Will we never learn the lesson?
We have so many *commonalities!*
Must we always seek out
what is different
so as to justify
the war cries we shout
deluding us to commit never-ending *brutalities*

Once Man was out of the cave
and enlightened by some *deity*
he concocted.... or uncovered
acclaiming this other god he discovered
just to head his personal religious *society*

All these differences invented
make us *forget*
that the colour of our blood
is the same, always *red!*
no matter how we pray
or how we are *bred*

whether Darwinian
or coming from the mud
or even survivors
and descendants from the Flood

Yet one single thing is both common and true
We are all of but a single *Humanity!*
So much else is merely delusional *vanity*
and when taken to extremes, brings only *insanity*

HUMANITY is the First Religion!
Only Humans can aspire to a *belief*
We must then embrace its first achievement,
that being HUMANE is its only commandment.
History has shown all the rest to bring *grief*

Pilgrimage
Carol Barrett

Mary, trace of blood tears on her face,
knows the glory of leaves, their lobes and veins.

This is a truth that accords with the journey:
in no two places are the leaves alike.

From Sydney she has traveled for the aspens,
blanket of sheer suns near Santa Fe.

A drought in Atlanta: maples drop without turning,
fall straight down, bypassing purgatory.

A funnel cloud in Kansas: elms splintered
will rot while standing, leaves sucked from their ears.

Cottonwood seeds burrow in the rubble,
grip what they can of soil, climb on spindly legs,

green-eyed walking sticks. Years will fall
before these limbs quaver, a flock of monarchs.

On a calendar she pencils in the White Mountains,
her arrival, timed to slip between winds,

that stillness at the far edge of the drop,
flash point when the dancer, leaping,

ascends the air, taut, before the legs
begin to think of folding, find the floor

before stubborn veins grace new snow,
shadowy imprint on hushed white shroud.

She is hunting near-death, navigating the globe
lugging her brown leather case.

Once I dabbled in leaves, pressed ruddy cheeks
of sugar maples between sheets of laid paper

with deckled edges. But this is devotion
of another order. Imagine the leaf watcher's

notebooks stacked on mahogany, swollen
like tiger lilies in the rain, the hands

of trees, fistfuls of death on every page, stolen
from hillside graves where the watchers

line up, a procession of celebrants. Witness
enough life curled up, able to fly,

and the burden lessens when your own
palms, wrinkled, sag at dusk, cherry wood,

or black walnut, waiting for the glory,
the chromatic of fall.

***

This poem was originally published in *Tiferet: Journal of Spiritual Literature*.
Reprinted with permission.

All Souls' Day
Lorraine Mangione

The souls, the souls, all the departed souls,
I live in them and they live in me,
especially now in November when the air is
thin and cold and I must wrap to keep warm.
I wrap in the souls but the cold finds its way
in through the tatterings of grand old scarves
and embroidered cloaks. You who have departed,
stay with me, I am not ready for your side,
leave me here with the glories of this world,
but stay with me even so, even if you must travel
far to the east in search of your new land.
Hold close to these threadbare arms.

For days now I am swamped in November spirit,
the spirit of those chosen few, lost to eternity.
Not allowed to live out our three score and ten.
Not even close. Not even close.
My Sister so thin, like the November branches
against the washed sky. Fighting for her life in November;
she went home as the year softened into Christ.
My Mother was always November, the gravity,
the mystery, the stripping away, the relentless truth.
And that sweet dark-eyed Child of God, born without
an ounce of this dark spirit within her.
Scourged until November claimed her.

I pray for each one, the interrupted souls,
I imagine their wringing of hands,
and I pray for more who join them, more who will join them,
the great train to heaven metaphor comes alive.
A prayer for myself, living so tenuously without them,
for the courage *to be here,* in November.
By the month's end utterly beaten down, desperate
for the light to come back, filled with the grimness of
stripped trees and gray skies. I walk with head down,
I can barely take in breaths, the air is so thin and the
gloom so complete. The pretense of color has evaporated.
The reign of bleak is upon us.

My Quiet Place/Further Meditations on My Quiet Place

Larry Graber

My Quiet Place

It's quiet in here
I can sense the subtlety
And feel the
closeness
Of my heart

There is a sad place
where sadness can live
and take a rest

No pressure
No expectations

Sadness
can rest its head
And just be

There are wounds here
But they are quiet now

I hold you, sadness,
by just letting go.

You have nothing
to fear or to do

you are sadness complete,
perfect the way you are

No shame
No performance

I feel only
Self-compassion

In this place

My quiet place

Further Meditations on My Quiet Place

I See u
in Your quiet place
Where time
Has its own meter

Rivers run open
Leaves fall
Free

A Floating
Canopy

Sustained
Motion

Varied
Together
Whole

Are they dancing?

Caking
Earth

Warm
Granite

Endless
Lines
Edged
In
Rocks
Repose

White
Noise

There
Is a bee
Buzzing
Somewhere

Perhaps
Long
Ago

Making its
Way

You
Can
Have
all
The
Time
You
Need

The
Leaves
Are your
Breath

You
Walk
With
Light
Feet

The
Earth
Knows
You

The Call of the Search
Shelley Pizzuto

I looked for you inside of me
I felt you there
You guided me here
I looked for you inside of me
I felt your breath
It was my air
I looked for you inside of me
You lit a fire
Seraphic desires
I looked for you inside of me
And you appeared
I asked to touch your heart in there
You said come sit, be still here
The light was bright, I lost all fear
I asked to root my soul and grow from here
I sit and look for you inside of me

The Anti-Christ
Candice Hershman

What if the Anti-Christ is this?

Anything you thought you should do
that derailed you from your heart's desire?

What of those times you wanted
to take off your clothes and run fast,
bounding like a dog into the sea,
throat bellowing a mayhem so signature,
you coined yourself your own unique,
amphibious species?

Have you ever walked out,
right in the middle of something you found shocking,
but perhaps the others kept silent,
either pursed their lips and looked
to each other cautiously
to measure their responses,
to gage for collective safety,
or perhaps looked down at their feet,
swallowed their protests hard
so that they would get an ulcer,
but you,
you sat up and said
"bull shit"
and walked out?

Did you ever let yourself get mad,
let yourself swear it,
narrowed your eyes into depth perception
so acute, it could see through armor
and into the soul of the betrayer,
thrown down your shield
and raised your honest outrage like a fist,
fighting more fairly and squarely
than those who never fight?

Have you ever loved somebody
you did not believe you should love,
beyond the rules, the grooming of
black tie and white lace dresses,
secretly, ardently, shameful
with your regrets split in two
between what you believed you should transcend
and trying to undo your heart
and throw it off like a mistake?

Other people's promises are strong.
They are made for us
and we believe and follow them
like lost sheep looking for a shepherd.
My God is not a Shepherd.
My God does not guide me into his path.
My God pushes me back to the world
without any answers,
pushes me back to my heart and tells me,
"look there, underneath the stones,
to the hot red clay of your heart
and shape it into what your feelings tell you.
I have given you the answer,
and the answer is yourself."

silly little buddha
Banu Ibaoglu Vaughn

I am thirsty, the body calls
Ringing in my ear- the sweet shopping lights
Hands shake with nerves and the blue light.
The distances near
The sirens get louder
The vistas draw me closer to my fear.
Then it's all gone
Tide has changed again
Was it even real?
How the fuck did I end up here?
Through some sick joke -
Some insistent space goddess watching, eating popcorn?
Can this really have sense?
Do I make it?
Do they give me?
Are the sages right?
Should I even listen?
Slap their words. non-sense.
It's all a conspiracy to trap the life and the light in their lap.
Then I skip.
Something soothes, the vistas open up again ever so softly, with their smiling gaze.
I smile like a silly little buddha.

Collecting Christian Sentiments
Louis Hoffman

This is not an anti-Christian or anti-religious poem; it is a witness to the destructive potential of any religious group that stands alongside its potential for good.

"Obviously all religions fall far short of their own ideals..."
~ Ernest Becker

Friends have said, I'm
A heathen, secular, a relativist
A pagan, lover of sin,
Too articulate, smug, arrogant
Worldly, of the flesh, and more
Deceiver and, the deceived
A wolf in sheep's clothing... a wolf

I've been told...
I'm avoiding responsibility
Leading the faithful astray
Thinking my way to hell
That I'm wrongheaded, pigheaded,
A hellmonger

I've been taught...
Compassion for sinners is sin
The Gospel is not love, but law
Grace was never intended for all
Education is dangerous, yet
Not as bad as thinking
Christian indoctrination and
Blind faith is the way

When I responded in like
My judgments and objections, I'm told
Were sin, a sign of the times...
Offering
The gift of martyrdom to this oppressed class
Most privileged of all people

I objected that their words seem sharp, then
A wise one explained these daggers were love
So I'm collecting Christian sentiments
Terms of endearment, letters of love
Assuring the good people will never cease
Praying for this compassionate soul
Lest my words, too, become flat, empty
Detached from feeling, devoid of love

Be Still
Michael E. Moats

Where do I go?
What do I do?
Is it enough?
Does it have to be?
Is it right?
Is it wrong?

"Be still."

...Be still? What?

"The busyness of others is of no concern to you.
Be still."

Hellfire and brimstone.
Sinner!
Hate the sin but love the sinner.

Mass shootings, gun violence.
Christians like guns.
If I have a gun I am being contradictory.

Do not go against the flow, or be labeled.

Sexual immorality.
It is the fault of gays and prostitutes.
Condemn them or condone them.

Do not go against the flow, or be labeled.

Focusing on the wrong things and losing sight of the problem
Noise, noise, and more noise.

Love your neighbor as you love yourself.
Do not be selfish.
Wait!
If I loved my neighbor as I loved myself, would I want to even be my neighbor?

If I support "the gays"
I am not being a good Christian.
Christ says to love others.
Stay true and do not falter,
or there is hell to pay.
Christ says He forgives.

Misguided imprints are understood in the head but contain fear in the heart.
They were given to me as a child,
and they have toiled with me as a plaything into my adult life.
Of Christ or of the world.
Right or wrong.
Good or evil.
Light or dark.
Where is there room for forgiveness, for me?

If I speak of Christ I am bombarded with ties to Fox News.
If I speak outside of the fortress of polarized belief I am called lost.

I try to love the world but get told I support hate and hypocrisy.
I try to hear my Christ,
But I get drowned out by my Christian brothers and sisters.
Do I belong?
Am I off track?
Will there be hell to pay?
Am I just a fool?

If I believe I am right I am told I am arrogant and prideful.
If I doubt I am wrong I am told I am a luke-warm Christian.
The world just tells me I'm wrong.
If I do nothing I feel helpless and drifting.
And yet, I hear, "Be still."

A whisper says, "walk with me."
Blaring loud speakers say to defend, protect, take up the fight.
I scream so loudly yet no one can hear.
My chest hurts from sternum to spine,
A hot coal searing my insides.

"Be still."

...But I must defend.

"Be still."

...But I must protect.

"Be still."

...But I must take up the fight.

A wind of rhetoric tells me to fight.
A wave of the world tells me I am blind and misguided.
A faceless voice that tells me to be still and to walk with Him feels comforting and confusing.

What I see in the world is too painful to hold.
If what I have read and have believed is true,
Then what I see and feel is only a glimpse
of what was on Your shoulders.

It's not rational, nor have You ever claimed to be.
The rational has only comforted me
in times of peacefulness and minor conflict.
Somehow "be still" seems to come
in times of great turmoil.

Tell me why I still doubt.
Tell me why I still find it easier to believe my colleagues' rational reasoning.
Tell me why I can't seem to let you go.
Tell me what to.......

"Be still."

...But I hurt so badly.

"I know.
Be still."

....

"Love."

"Love."

"Love."

I Pray for Scars *for my sister*
Richard Bargdill

I pray for scars
because so far
so many wounds
have not healed.

I seem to think
that these holes
cut in my soul
should somehow
be sown by now.

These bumps and bruises,
cuts and contusions
in reality, may be,
deeper than they
first seemed to me.

All things grow
even neglected so.
Some things grow
best in the dark:
like secrets and lies.
Hidden potatoes, too,
grow eyes.

But, painful memories
continue to thrive
and what's worse
is they hurt like a curse
that gains more strength
than it had at first.

Like all wounds,
these need our care,
to remove infection
and allow repair.
We rinse off the dirt,

push out puss, use band-aids
and ointments to cover them up.

When I take off the wrappings
And look where those wounds are,
I pray for myself
that I only see scars.

An Empty Soul
Steve Fehl

It is said that God cries; yet, I am not moved.
It is said that God sees; yet, I am not seen.
It is said that God speaks; yet the words have no meaning.
It is said that God is; yet I am not.

My soul is empty, it is but a void.
My heart beats faintly, as a dry well in a wasteland.

The lights shine brightly, tree branches filled with sparkles and twinkles.
The air is teeming with music, tones of laughter, and themes of hope rule.
Images of warmth and closeness abound, but...

I cry, and there are no tears.
I see, but there is no vision.
I speak, and the words fall mute
I am, but have no faith,

My soul is empty and dark,
My heart is as a dry well.
My body is limp.
My spirit grasps for breath.

If God cries, does he experience my pain?
If God sees, does she recognize my anguish?
If God speaks, does he know I am lost?
If God is, is she aware I am also?

When my soul is dark and empty, faith brings no hope.
When my spirit is gasping for breath, belief gives no life.

Have I missed the glory? Will I miss the glory?
Oh, please, do not let me miss the glory; please do not let me miss the light.

When my soul is void and empty I am blinded from the glory.
When my spirit gasps for breath the light is dim and fading.

Please, do not let me miss the glory, nor lose the glowing light.

When my life is limp and hopeless, keep the glory within my sight. When my heart is aching and its beat is fading, keep the light burning and help me focus on its flame.

My soul is empty, oh, how I desire the glory and the light.

Sacrifice at Eleven Years Old
Erica Loberg

It's lunchtime
I don't get excited
I get ready
To feel pride
And young hope.

I genuflect and enter being good
God is good
And I will hear him, find him, even if I have to sacrifice recess.

Because that takes me one step closer to that place everyone seems to be
He stands before the meek lunch congregation and he is so close
He says the sermon like the sky is blue.

But I want God
I want him to talk to me
What does it take to find him?
Church, bible reading, my knees on the pew hurt so bad that it has to bring something

Magic.

I chew gum in class
I pass notes
A future of failure awaits those that don't adhere to demands
"You'll get extra credit if you attend mass during lunch."
So I sit front and center
I don't need any extra credit but want to make sure if I do, I'll get it

Education is knowledge only brought forth through God
So I go to church.

Being mean to my little sister needs to change
I need something to help my natural inclination to yell at her when she crosses the line that separates her side of the room from mine.

I do the rosary before bed
I look at the drawing that was passed out in religion class
I stayed between the lines
Mary of Guadeloupe looks so peaceful
I'll find that peace
Keep doing the entire rosary
That's ten hell Mary's
Not eight.

He offers the Eucharist
The body of Christ, Amen
I want to eat a whole stack of it
I wonder if priests do that behind closed holy doors.

I hear the mesh of boys playing kickball, handball, basketball, volleyball, and can imagine the girls standing in the corner talking to form stronger cliques and I smile
Leaving me estranged
They are weak
Church will give me something
I hope
It has to
The idea of church not doing anything
For me
Never crosses my mind
Six weeks of sacrifice must work.

I walk into a church now and feel nothing
There is nothing there

After all those lunches.

Taking the Prayers Back
Candice Hershman

I felt my grandmother say "I'm sorry" tonight.
She said -
"I did not know until I was dead."

Strong thighed women pray
with the pound of their feet
into the ground,
the ecstatic rotations of their posteriors,
hands pushing the sky back up
to make room for their heads
while they swing back and forth
on the grace of their necks.

People pass
or even brush up to each other
in brief, unobliged interface,
swaying and then pulsing out
- joy -

I want to know,
why didn't we pray this way
when we were young?
Why were we told
that prayers lived in our brains?
That wishes are plans?
That blessings are earned like points?

We earn ourselves
when we step through the door
with our bodies,
the gateways of heaven on our mouths,
and here in the dance,
sometimes I stop to sit,
to let my breath do its two-step,
so excited
with a kiss perched upon my lips,
the heat of limbs generated,
so then I look over and there is

nobody to give the kiss to,
and at least a half dozen
who I would choose.
But that's the thing:
people are moments
stretched into manageable lifetimes
and I want
to be in the moment,
or have the moment in me:
next to the dance,
this is an exalted prayer.

Why did you tell me not to dance?
Why did you tell me
that I would lose my honor?

I move with violent peace.
The God dimension is there,
the bass an entry way
and there are so many doors that I pass,
others moving with violent peace,
our eyes meeting,
sometimes turning away and back in,
and sometimes returning a smile,
but moving about,
the air so thick with music,
the room becomes an ocean
and we are moving buoyantly,
just shy of flight.
Everyone can hear this
the way the deaf
place their hands to the ground.

When I am done,
I wonder what mistakes I will make,
what the next generation will need
in order to pray.
I imagine ancestors
dancing a jitterbug dance with the young.
If I would have known sooner,
I would have taken my children

to a church that danced.
I know,
someday I will say "I'm sorry:
I did not know until I was dead."

Lost and Found
Emily Lasinsky

You led me to search for God,
Said you needed to find yourself.
As you made your way toward heaven,
I went through hell.
Years of silence helped me learn that to truly enter heaven, one
 has to go through hell.
I don't know where you are and what stairways you've
 climbed,
But my hope for you is that in the process of finding,
You lost yourself.

And all the angels say,
"Amen."

Made in the Image
Dakota Gundy

Divine Beings full of potential, I am, you are, we all are "Made in the image of God."

Genesis...creation, new beginnings and God said "It was good."

Man created a god in his own image, placing fear and guilt in the wake of the "followers."

Man created religions with the intention of manipulating people for power and control.

"Thou shalt not have any other idols (gods) before Me."

Man built himself as the idol (god) of Christianity with judgment, discrimination, exclusion of different people based on many different reasons.

Man-made religion depersonalizing others to make them less than to help appear powerful and all knowing.

War is waged in the name of god,

God is of peace and love for all because we were made in the image of God.

We are the God spark in our hearts.

War is man-made through ego and driven by psychosis.

Wait, Stop! The God I know is love, nothing else, no anger, no conditions, UNCONDITIONAL LOVE.

Stop the hate crimes, the religious pious actions that demean others in the name of god.

Man-made religion is what creates atrocities, hate crimes, discrimination of other groups.

Peace, Divine Love, unconditional love and complete acceptance that is my understanding of God.

Divine Beings full of potential, I am, you are we all are "Made in the image of God."

Genesis...creation, new beginnings.

Prayer
Edward Korber

I pray for u,
all the Xs the Ys
and for ours children's future.
For any 1 who ever felt alone,
To everyone who ever felt disowned,
i pray for u and my country i call home,

i pray for u and me listener
 so listen up my brother and sister
Just take a deep step back and imagine a much bigger picture
cuz i cry the so real hoping u hear my appeal
i pray for those inner city street kids struggling to find their place
In a curial social world too concerned with race, state and place

Yes i pray of you, my soap opera
about single mommas and the papas
about the struggle, the hustle and troubles of this living city
And the need for compassion and pity
Filled with empty bellies rumbling but still humble
despite silent earthquakes that sometimes make us fall to our knees

we still are defying the odds
hungry like young golden eagles
Singing to God
"Lord give us the strength to carry on"

so yes i pray
 for you and me the true blue
cause I fight to redefine our (the) stars
hoping to get this trickled down soul song through
too the unlocked doors of your pensive and eternal Heart

i wanna spark your world and get things reborn from its ashes
i wanna un-fog all our perceptual glasses
and make us see all of gods, the creative sons and daughters
Yes, the ones society abandoned to be its bastards
knowing that that despite this we still grow and go
Though so often we might move through this life like thick molasses

i point to the north and south like a true compass
East and west trying to climb the spiritual fences
Please just follow the sounds of this heralding trumpet
listen up cause you see
i write these for the love, agape

For any 1 who ever felt alone, any1 who ever felt disowned or downhearted,
i pray for our countries
the ones we call our homes
i cry out for u listener so come hither brothers and sisters
take a step back and see the depth of our big picture
 listen up, hear my appeals cuz i write and pray for you, the real deal

Prayer in Poetry
Yasna C. Provine

I'm only as small as my thoughts suggest,
and what work it is to stretch them
into fibers of a quilt
that's expansive enough
to warm a galaxy lit up by stars
and vacuums of space and timelessness.

I want to tuck God into bed at night,
kiss His face
instead of rolling beads of the Holy Ghost
strung across a rosary
or polishing a crown of thorns adorning a blackened crucifix.

I want to know the things I only quietly think
after the fact.
I want to live what's hidden
beneath the sheer heavy veils of
my lidded dreams.

I want Truth to be as concrete as
depth of sin
and as humbling as
good deeds.

I want to be all of what is enough,
no less,

but maybe more

if it suits my flawed way of being.

I'm only as strong as my world encourages.

And, oh,
how painful it is to be stripped and taunted
by love.

How beautiful it is to be reduced

to verses of poetry
        bleeding into the most somber of symphonies.

My emotions,
broken and shrunken,
sit fragile like pages of scripture.
My resolve fits there,
as perfectly as irony does
in the Good News of tiny Bible print.

Salvation makes no sense
because confusion makes the world go 'round.

But, my God,
I am something miraculous!

I'm a glimmer of light in your all-seeing eye.

I move softly,
like the breath of an unanswered prayer
swirling through centuries
of white knuckles,
coincidences,
past lives,
and perfect timing.

My wings grow big. My wings fold small.
I am only as heavenly
as these gusts of wind lift me.

My divinity is an earthly practice.

In the Trenches
Sean Gunning

The hip young priest in the long white robe
is tall and broad shouldered. Wisconsin strong.

"All war is about deception....
Are we at war sisters and brothers?
Are we?"

Are you kiddin' me?
Sun Tzu. The Art of War.
And what's with the iPad?

"YES!
YES WE ARE AT WAR!"
he roars towards a teenager
seated near the side exit door.
"WHO ARE WE AT WAR WITH JASON?"

Jason's answer is muffled,
as if given across a battlefield.

Through a mic at his cheek
hanging like a "j"
Wisconsin strong shakes
the rows of cheap chandeliers,
the bell in the bell tower,
and the people in the pews:
"YES!
SATAN!
WE ARE AT WAR, SISTERS AND BROTHERS!
WE NEED TO WAKE UP AND FIGHT!"

A fifteen-minute barrage of
old-school revivalist fire and brimstone fury
ricochets from tabernacle
to quivering Sanctus bell,
words exploding like sacramental bombs,
shocking his flock from the path of sin and apathy
that leads to Hell.

Okay, I get it.
The devil is alive and strong.
We have to guard against his ways.

But in war, What's right? What's wrong?

How do I read an Afghani's gaze?

How on this blessed earth
do we get along with those who want us dead,
and would kill our children
and our children's children too?

Is it truly wrong, to lead Army Strong,
with God's avenging sword,
as your apostle did for you?

Forgiveness won't stop a roadside bomb.

You know there's dark and light;
what's been lost and won....

You know *what I've done....*

I go back in nineteen days.
You know how many lives depend on me....

Jesus, please...
I'm on my knees...
I need your eyes in mine to help me see.

Please bring us all *safely home;* us and them....

Dulce et decorum non est *pro patria mori.*

***

Previously published in *Cadence Collective*. Reprinted with permission.

Absolute
Tracy Lee Sisk

This poem was written in response to a brief connection with my dear one as we shared our love for the last time.
For Grandma and Granddad ~ I will love and miss you always.

"I wish I could believe what she believed", he said to me during our last visit.

What do I say as he referred to his love of 75 years?

I could not, I would not say that she and he would be apart for eternity.

What, fill his last days with more misery and heartache? ~ His heart shattered the moment she died!

No more sorrow or anguish to your soul, only space to be with the one love of your life.

Granddad, what you want and believe will be.

Together for eternity.

No separation.

Your soul, your heart, your essence is freed for whatever is next ~ I'll see you at my time.

I could not, I would not, I am absolute to never again.

Oh, How I Wish
Steve Fehl

Oh how I wish I was handsome, virile, and graceful;
    But instead I am frumpy, heavy, and clumsy.

Oh how I wish I was intelligent, wise, and insightful;
    Instead I am slow, confusing, and dense.

As I meander through my days surrounded by the brilliant and beautiful;
    I wonder what it is like to be smart or popular or desired.

I wonder and I meander . . .
    . . . with no sense of purpose . . .
    . . . with no sense of presence . . .
    . . . with no sense of desire . . .
    Lost, alone, detached, and rejected.

I know I ought not compare myself, but I do
    And I never measure up.
    I come up short . . .
    . . . sometimes third,
    . . . sometimes last,
    . . . sometimes not at all.

Oh, how I wish . . .

Soul Sisters

Nesreen (Alsoraimi) Frost

Swirled around
and twisted into
My own strands
of spiritual DNA
I feel and relate
with your laugh
with your pain
Can wink
at the seductress
My heart warms
with the nurturer, the healer
Delve into the mind
that I admire and respect
Can joke
with the child
And share in our essence
Most beautiful
In its real, uncovered and natural state
Daydreams and neurotic tales
Of the future,
present and past
Protecting our sacred feminine
Projecting whatever the moment
calls for
Unapologetically
Because judgment doesn't live here
And compassion is strong
When applied to the self and the other
Daughters and mothers
We share energy
We embrace
With our words
With our silence
With our solidarity

Revelation
Nick Owen

Sometimes
Time slips its moorings
The world is ocean once again
Omnipotent
Omnipresent
Engulfing

The golden eagle of my dreaming spheres
Suddenly seven shades of black
Become a crow
A black, black crow
Upon my neck

Waves of grief
Break over boughs
Black skies
A torrent of tears, interminable
Crash in upon my ark of hope
Graves yaw and pitch and broach
Roll, heave through seas of time
Vomiting up their blemished
Beautiful bones

The dead break back
Through sodden slabs of stone
And cloying clay clods
Headstones bouldered, broken
Caked with grime
Cannot hold back this
The end of time

A flood of feelings
Drives me through the sunken trees
A blue jay fledgling
Dying at my feet
Is breathing still
A life not yet complete

A burst of pity quells my odd disgust
Asks, must I kill it?
Yes, I know I must.

The booted universe comes down upon its head
And even then the creature is not fully dead
The eggshell brain is crushed
But still I see
Another breath, before the spirit
Can, at last, go free

The seven seals stay sealed
No ugly horsemen yet have passed this way
The tides are ebbing
And, in spite of its decay
My own life
Has not slipped away today

But soft is the kiss of the crow
Touches me deep
Perhaps tonight I'll find
Profound refreshing sleep
Perhaps tomorrow
I won't need to weep

I leave my golden angel dog to haunt my dreams
I walk my happy black dog
In and out of lovely streams
Where black birds, warblers, robins sing
Above the babbling river
On its bed of stones
Sitting on an island
All is blue and gold and green again
Within my magic circles, fiery gold,
Where glorious Gryphons guard the gates
And heron, whores and Goddesses
Protect the doors
And human headed hares
Patrol the earth
I write

Of the apocalypse
The end of days

A golden angel smiles on me
From way on high
For I have had a dream
And I shall tell it to you
Bye and bye

Revelation
Eschatology
Crow flies free

Nurturer of Spirits
Natalia Mello

My God too is a reflection of my flesh
Or better yet me of she
Who spread her knees hesitantly to bare me
From the warmness of her womb
Into the chilling of this reality
She tries to warm when she breathes
The summer breeze.

My literal creator
And upon my arrival she on her knees
Prayed for my salvation
Since the day of my creation
For truth she knew.

She for centuries the roots of humanity
Spreading her hair and digging into the soil of our souls
As the veins that carry the blood to my fingertips
She brings the color to the cheeks of existence
at sunset.

Like the most voluptuous and fruitful of trees
She provides emotional shade for eternity
And in the holy river that runs from her eyes
Sometimes when she cries
For her daughters that die
Or who live as they are dead
In that river I bathe.

Mother of all
A reflection of she
Pure energy
Look up and her beauty is what blinds your eyes
Too great to look at without guise
So at times she must hide.

She feeds the sun
That kisses the shoulders of everyone
Despite the engulfing darkness

Its light permeates
Through every corner of emptiness
It radiates.

And only when we die can we lie
With eyes wide open to the sky
From which the spirit is liberated
And returns home to her womb
The most forgiving tomb.

Despite the times we call out
Her name in vain
Her essence runs through my veins
Despite the defilement
Of the walls of her body
In which we tear with false images of beauty
How often we suffocate her soul's flame
Under the blanket of misogyny
Her throat bleeds and her voice strains
With the gags of patriarchy
We cut her limbs out of existence
That are the wolves and the trees
But still she forgives completely.

Her love is heavy
It cannot be bothered
Her belly grows
And from it is born laughter and dance
Her eyes cry so that the rivers and oceans do not dry
But waters of joy would quench our sorrows
The truly divine mother.

So under the moon my soul moves for her
I worship her entirely
And all that carry her feminine energy
She, She, me a reflection of she
She and me
I realize
The tears fall too from my eyes
That I am she and she is me
At times forced into darkness

She is my core
So deep
Yet beyond me infinitely.

Strangers
Michelle Sideroff

I do not know who you are anymore,
As I sit here by this empty chair crying.
I lost so much and my spirit is in mourning.
And to feel that I have also lost you is trying.

From when I was knee-high I followed you,
And practiced the guiding words of the lord.
Righteously, being a part of what you do,
As my creator and protector of my world.

Every night on bended knees I prayed,
Hoping for health, guidance, and love.
Convictions and dedication did not sway,
As I sent my faith and fate to you above.

The world from church to town changed before my eyes,
Pain and loss chiseled at my innocence, it soon faded away.
No responses come to my queries and my voice slowly dies.
Unstable ground rattles and lures me to temptation's sway.

Hymns no longer escape my lips nor are prayers said.
My knees will no longer bend nor do my hands rise.
Instead, I search for you in the communion of bread.
I reach out for you in the holy waters I was baptized.

The lost parts did not begin with faith, but within me.
I changed in my losses and it rippled onto my beliefs.
Murky shadows of pain hid the truth I couldn't see.
That I was lost to me and that I seek you out in relief.

I do not know who we are anymore for we have changed.
I descend from blind devotion toward a mindful view.
I relinquish the old doctrines and welcome the strange,
As I sit here in this pew, praying and holding the new you.

Abhidharma
Katherine Kreil-Sarkar

This illusionary play
exposes the very limits
of my faiths, my duty.
You caution five great fears
I conquer, I conquer not.
I fear to speak, to be known,
to stand naked in judgment
in front of those assembled.
In front of those divided, who plot
my destruction, the defiling
of my name, of all I built up.
Lest I be plunged into despair,
detachment
disillusionment
delirium
deeper
until I find myself alone
Unsupported, unwelcome
My family struggles
I seek their safety, health
to fill their emptiness
crumbling, decay, silence
I stumble
You are not there
I call out
You answer not
I fear silence
You are silent
I am silent
I am motionless
I am still
I am not

You answer... All five fears?
Not one you escaped?

Already Lost
Jyl Anais Ion

I've lost you   already
just after I found you, again,
this time,
and here we are or rather   there you are, on that
rocky, ragged terrain,
near, where my blood first spilled onto the earth,
   this time, this life.
And here I am on this strange expanse of land
that juts into the ocean erect.

But you found her, the one you'd been looking for
all your life. And she isn't me.
You found her
and now, your heart is occupied,
your life colonized and I can't have you
even though you say I can.
That's not what I want.
Not that way.

I don't want to own you.
I want to love you,
But I need you here with me, whole,
and focused, in the flesh.
But you're not.
Instead I hear you speak to me
in the ether
and I feel you nearby, close,
with an awareness that surrounds me like
a cloak of protection.   I am safe.
I say, come closer.
Come inside. In the dark.

I just found you, again.   Finally,
after how long, I don't know.
And my words
when I extend them
have met with silence,
an absence I regret,

after which I want to put the words   back
into my mouth, take them back with my hands,
pull them back into my   heart.

Are you waiting   for me
to recover?
I'm waiting for that,   too.

I miss you already.
I miss you. I miss you.

This is the longing,
the angst I tried to avoid.
I am already lost.

In Darkness Lives...
Lorraine Mangione

The forest is filled with
the ends of things.
Thin black branches of fir
crack with a crisp shout
as I gather wood for kindling.
Decay of old stumps
diagonally seared–
some smoothed with age
some blood-letting in their rawness.
Fragments of splintered wood
timeworn, rainworn,
mouldering into the earth.
Whole great trees downed
and screaming into mournful
postures of spent lovers
and withered age.
With careful step I
wind a pathway through
this menagerie of
tortured sculptings.
The foreignness of such
violence ends in a
shudder within.
Sojourn for renascence
becomes an unsought for
meeting with how things end.
Ramble through forest
in search of a view
is now a question of survival.
These woods have swindled me,
these trees betrayed me,
offering no glimpse of skylight,
giving only the haunting netherside.

Late night at my camp
I sit entranced
by ashes still glowing
chunks of wood ever burning.

Points of light hold back
the spectral patterns
of forest night,
draw me in from
the creaking black
all encompassing.
Tiny furnace under
a moonless sky.
I sit in forest stillness.
I crouch in the stillness
of one hoping for a birth.
I sit small in the
stillness of a catacomb
at midnight.
With stick in hand
I stir the ashes,
and watch the spurt
of a single flame.

It's Personal
Nathaniel Granger, Jr.

I sometimes wonder
If I am hallucinating
Because I love my God
I browbeat you not
To believe as I do
I thank Him for his love.

You don't know my story
Of why I give Him glory
And so perhaps neither do I
I do know
That He's been good
Hinder me not as I give Him praise.

Now don't get me wrong
I am far from perfect
No faking it
Overcoming my sins
Ensures I can win
I thank Him for his grace.

I sometimes wonder
If I am hallucinating
For feeling the "what" I feel
Right or wrong, it's not my intent
To feel His presence
I thank Him for his mercy.

And so you'd rather
Sit back and judge
We all fall short; No shit's fragrant
He too has peered through the windows
Of your glass house
You gossip; I'll pray.

You say you have religion
Nowadays 'tis spiritual
Help me understand

How is that working
Apart from relationship
I thank Him for being real.

I sometimes wonder
If I am hallucinating
Dreaming of everyone liking this poem
S'posing wishful thinking
Having been blessed,
There's no room for stress
I thank Him for who He is to me.

        ---It's personal.

The Stars Speak
Erica Palmer

If I walk out in the night, and can't see the stars,
Are you there? Can you see me?

If I walk out in the night, and feel the wind on my face,
Are you there? Can you feel me?

If I walk out in the night, and I scream,
Would you care? Could you hear me?

If I walk out in the night, and just keep on walking,
Would you walk with me?

The stars tell me you're there.
I can't see you.

The stars say that you care.
I can't feel you.

The wind whispers you exist.
I can't know you.

My search is never-ending.
Who will save me?

Hope lives only
When the stars speak.

Autobiography
Keaneasha Garcia

Straight out a movie
Straight off a shelf
Religious leader obsessed with wealth

Secrets mixed with
God and Glory
Stephen King wrote my life story

Chains
Tasers
Paintballs
Whips
Married women turned into pulpit tricks

Church and Scandal
God and Grief
Patiently waiting to be set free

Something's not right
I noticed it young
Told to keep quiet
"Haters" were shunned

The sheep were deceived
The leader intact
Who answers for this when Jesus comes back?

Blood-stained hands
Precious pearls
The tormented soul of a once young girl

Picture perfect exterior
But damaged within
When did prostitution in the church begin?

No judgement here we were all led blind
Robbed of freedom, family, money, and time

Precious seconds lost
Years gone to waste
At the age of 18
I changed my fate

Got out of that place
Found God for myself...
Learned he's not concerned with material wealth

But rather a rich spirit
The kind that makes devils flee
But learn for yourself
Don't just take it from me

Deceived by a shepherd
In this wretched world
God save the soul
Of this once young girl

Blood-stained hands
Precious pearls
A glimpse into the life
Of this once young girl

Perpetual Motion
Kat V. Rosemond

The grim shadows of dreamscape
Took hold with sharp claws
Shook and cut Zebra
To her core

Every dark specter
That had wounded her heart
From her beginnings
Those remembered
Those forgotten
Rose up before her
From out of the deep abyss
From amnestic depths
Of underground ruined chambers
Looming
Groaning
Choking her throat

Troubled soul
She woke in the grass
With the storm howling
Deep within
A searing menacing voice
Growled low
Told her she was alone
Abandoned
Doomed

Her body
felt so heavy
So burdened
scarred
Belly pierced and torn
Her heart
Cold painful lead
Can it bear another beat?
Can she draw another breath?

She is trapped
In the shadowy dungeons
Corners of horror
Deep in her guts
So many wounds
So much fear and despair
Her guts shout of the violence
In their pain
The spew of their stew

But Zebra yet has fire
In her spirit
Though it feels like
A dim ember
She stands on her legs
Feet penetrating
Imprinting the mud
Her primal signature

She cries aloud
To the Heavens above
To the white banners
Flying against the deep blue
To the Spirit above
In the Kingdom of Light

Far to the West
She looks to the mountain
In the distance she sees him
Her Shaman King
He is far away
Yet she can feel his voice
Reminding her...

She breathes
A long deep breath
Hearing his wisdom
Her body resonates
Shadows are teachers
Shadows are gifts
Do not be afraid

To face the abyss
You are never alone
Open up your being
And discover the wisdom

And then there is silence
Emptiness
The canvas awaits
The first brush stroke
A star alights
In Zebra's heart
And its glow
Gives warmth
And freedom

And then Zebra feels it
The rhythm
The pulse of her heart
The waves of her breath
The wings of the wind
The dance of the trees
And the grasses
The flight of the crows
And the vultures
Mother Earth's heartbeat
Sun and Moon's orbits

The Spirit speaks
And Zebra knows
For the first time
She is not trapped
She is no captive
She is no victim
There is no stuck
There is always movement
No matter how small

She knows now
She feels now
She is always in movement
With each pulse

With each breath
With each step

Her legs find their strength
The mud on her feet is sublime
She is not afraid
She is not alone
Her wings now spread wide
Her belly is moving
Through pain and through healing
She will know the abyss
As well as the light
And her spiral
Is timeless
In perpetual motion

"Immaculate Combustion"
Joshua Ferguson

Immaculate Conception
Is nothing more than
Spontaneous combustion
The Big Bang is coming again
The verse will come full circle
Before bursting inward into oblivion
Wishing on the moon
A new star is born
A new universe is scorched
As a little earth floats around
Another birth of another world war
Portable poetry printed panoply
Passing propaganda para problema
The plan is etched in the volcanoes
The passage twisted in the tornadoes
As the blacklist broadens so rapidly
Contempt of patriotism, consent
Contempt of humanity, consent
Contempt of nationalism
Consent to contempt of unity
Lost in the studio of the loyalist party
Forgotten dossier, forgotten identity
Walk down the aisle
Join the silenced and the censured
It's all uphill from here
As the shadows of the giants keep stretching
The light of oneness still shedding
Entirely surrounded,
They stand in the upright brigade
Entirely enlightened,
There's no choice but to crusade
This is the song of immaculate conception
Sing to the tune of spontaneous combustion

Spirituality
David Bentata

The Wise One arrived in solemn silence
His talk would be on "Self Spirituality"
a popular one these *days*
when all quote that melodic *phrase*
yet none understand it in reality

It was packed, standing room only
So the Wise One asked for extra chairs
that were stacked *outside*
and off they all went to *provide*
a seat for each one from downstairs

And when all were seated he began
"We are made up of two parts
conflicting, competing until *death*
an internal battle till our last *breath*
Spirit and Animal with but one heart."

"Tonight I have seen you all very clearly!
To find comfort was your sole intention
So you each did Animal *work*
each getting his own chair with a *smirk*
Each his own Animal despite your pretension"

"Now if you were truly as Spiritual as you claim,
if you had let your Spirit guide you,
you would have still brought up a *seat*
but given it to your friend as a *treat*
That would've been a Spiritual breakthrough"

"Though the action remains the same
one is done by you for the Animal part
To satisfy your "self" was the *intention,*
instead the Spirit requires *abstention*
till you share with your fellow man ......
..............................your Spiritual Heart"

Spirit and Stardust
Carrie Arnold

Under twinkling stars
And illuminated wings
A broken spirit was revealed
Accidentally, or with celestial purpose

Brotherly love, selflessly shared
Safe, protective arms
Gently, patiently
Offered refuge for this damaged soul

Hours of pain
Years of shame
Evaporated into the stardust
Offering a glimpse of wholeness in its place

Temptation
Carol Barrett

Bringing you a handful of raspberries
I lifted a child's offering to your own
pale fist, stirring the colander,

cheese cloth already the color of jam,
the air acrid with sweet pulp. Raspberry
is the only stain that stays, will not

purple in the evening light, seeds hard
as mustard. I remember the froth pinking
at the edges, as if making cotton candy

and snow cone, the warning it would burn
my tongue salt red. We stay such impulses
with trial: stained hands return

to the berry patch, ripe lobes falling
from pith. The young hold to the stem,
squeeze honeycomb cells, while sparrows

drop seedy pink splotches on the drive.
I make another hollered entrance through
the kitchen door, soaked with fruit,

mouth fuschia with discovery, your apron
billowing for a damp hand, its exquisite
cherry joy. Thus we learn the plump

lessons of the vine, the urge to gulp,
the raspberry smell of savor. Jelly
cools beneath a creamy paraffin lid.

In the glass: our berried youth.

***

"Temptation" was originally published in *The Christian Century* in 2003. Reprinted with permission.

Prayer
Matthew D. Eayre

I don't know what I pray to,
But I know there's something there.
More than me, more than blood and electricity,
More than stone and sand
I say, lead me, show me, and bring me.
I pray, use me, guide me, and help me.
I don't know why I pray
But at least I'm hearing my prayer.
There's only now, time is a lie,
 Straight lines don't exist,
Past and future are the same, imaginary
I don't know how I keep praying,
But I know that it's not fair.
Life has two meanings, to see and to be seen
Perception of truth creates the dishonest story I tell
I don't know where my prayers go,
But I hope they arrive there.

Life is a Contradiction in Terms
Richard Bargdill

Life is a forgetting, it's a learning,
It's a forgetting what you've learned.

It's being poor, it's being wealthy,
Neither necessarily pertaining to money.

Life is who you are, it's who you're becoming,
It's also who you are not.

It's ambiguous, definitive, arbitrary, and concrete
and concrete is something that always cracks.

Life is clear and vague, sunshine and rain
      sometimes doing both on the same day
Nothing is more important than our weather.

It's what you need that is exactly what you can't give,
and also that which prevents you from receiving.

Life is a song you make up
      and can not remember the words.
A feeling you search for but it is ahead of you
      behind you, maybe you trip on it,
One sad-blissful moment.

It's a magic trick that you try to figure out,
      on the tip of your tongue,
Only to fade like a dream,
      into the garbage disposal of consciousness.

Life is a pattern, a path, the road
      you thought you were following, trying
To get to the middle of nowhere,
      but you know you are off center,
Someone has already been there cutting down the trees.

It's a cadence, a rhythm, a rhyme
      But suddenly-- What's the next line?

The toes are tapping--
    How strange to find them rapping out of time.

Life is a sore pain that feels good.
    A pure pleasure, those are rare,
A pleasurable pain, all are different,
    yet undifferentiated.

It's never as bad as it seems,
    nor depressing as it sounds.
A pin to prick your bubble,
    Stairs take you up when down.

Life is provocative, boring,
    positivity and negativity
We must know with whom we should be,
    hopefully ourselves.

It's a bunch of adjectives strung together
Trying to make sense, but failing. A dangling participle.

Life means trying to find good soil,
    stretching your roots over rocky terrain.
It's overcoming both the climate and stretch marks
    of your youth and growing toward the light.

You can learn a lot from a rock,
    and a tree, a weed, a seed,
The sea, waves, catching the greens
    as you drive,
From another, occasionally, a kiss.
    These are raw moments
But it can't always be raw,
    we need time to heal
We are sensitive
    under all these calluses.

Life is a clay to be molded that has already been shaped
    Sometimes we can only remodel what is laid
If we are up for the work, take out the walls, fix the roof
    Sand blast the sides, re-furbish,

re-finance, re-discover
>   Our foundations, then add another room.

It's a skin to be worn, ripped and torn,
>   fore-sakened, forlorned,

Celebrated on the day we were born,
>   Then shed, molted, left withered today

As we slither away.

It's the straight and narrow only for a while
>   The road veers, the river meanders

Our thought curves, and even turns back on itself.

Life is a restriction, a constriction,
>   a grasping, a letting go,

Attachment, detachment, uprooting,
>   undermining, undercutting,

A lifting the legs to vacuum underneath.

It's a talking to yourself when the conversations good,
>   It's being silent when one's song is playing,

Saying more than you said, saying more than you should.
It's the last second score,
That slow coming train,
That special stone
That you kicked then picked
Up.

Life is a smile, a frown, maybe a smirk.
A chuckle to yourself which no one else will appreciate.
No one. That's nice.

It's that night you didn't do what you should have done
>   but actually did much more.

It's beautiful, ugly, weak and strong,
We might say an awkward beauty.

It's hearing, seeing, touching, losing
>   all your senses, becoming

Blind, deaf, senseless.

       Then regaining your sensibilities,
Your sense/abilities, your sense of ability.

It's having some thing to say, having it
       All come out backwards, sidewards, dribble.
Sometimes it comes out perfect,
       Hair stands up! Eyes Drool!

Life is self-deception, self-exploration,
       lies and truth, where the truth lies.
Truth can only be swallowed in small doses
       like a kernel.

Life is a death, many deaths,
       the small death, the big death,
The death of you as you know yourself
       in more ways than one.

It's a gathering, a separating
You can lose by winning, and succeed in your losses.

It's when the "you" becomes "I"
When "they" becomes no one
And you are alone amongst
the Masses.

It's a hiding and a showing and being afraid to show.
The light can be oppressive, there are friends
       among the shadows.
It's the inside and the outside,
       Both can be prisons and the keys
to yourself are just out of reach
       under your nose.

It's hearts high, then smashed
Hearts are more like fine glass than we think
Love grows like a weed on the street
In the cracks of that which is concrete.

Life is a long story, poem, or project,
But despite its length is unfinished,
some detail
              escaping,
                        elusively,
                                  dancing......

Moon Half-Full
Sean Gunning

From the bucket-seat of a low to the ground
classic black Series 62 Cadillac
convertible with red leather seats,
tailfins, and the windows rolled down,
parked in a city called Orange
at 2:45 in the afternoon,
a flawless sapphire sky is made more perfect
by a Leroy-was-here half-moon
sliced from 10 to 4,
the way a poem is made more perfect
when tainted by human imperfection.

The fully ascended sun — too powerful
to be ascribed a color or shape —
perpetually blazing upon
our beautiful blue and green world,
laves in absolute light the shimmering fronds
of the Queen palms lining the strip-mall parking lot,
firing their impossibly tall trunks
higher and thinner,
as if heaven-bound.

And there's the American
and Russian rocket-ships
racing to the moon;
and me, seven-years-old,
in front of a black and white T.V.
the size of a shoebox
in a terraced house in West London,
wondering why so much money
was being misdirected
when so many children
were starving in Africa.

And the other day, when my American wife
said the space race was
a "worthwhile human endeavor,"
all I could think of was how amazing life is

when two people can have
such different understandings
of what God wants of us,
and still be devoted to Him/Her.

And just now, on my mobile,
the nice man from the vinyl record shop
apologizing for the delay in getting back to me;
explaining his girlfriend dumped him
a week before he was going
to ask her to marry him, and broke his heart.
But he's not sleeping in his car anymore,
because he found a friend's garage to live in…
so things are looking up.

Life
Steve Fehl

Each day, as the sun begins to rise, one more time we enter the fray.
We struggle, we fight, and we wrestle with all our might,
just hoping that we stay alive.

As the sun begins to set, we settle in feeling completely spent.
The struggle was hard, the fight was tough,
and all we are left with is our thoughts.
Thinking of what it means to live ... or die.
We ask ourselves if it is worth the fight,
Or might it be better to perish and escape the blight.

But as each day comes and goes, we continue our battle to beat our demise
Never stopping to realize that one of these days we shall succumb,
and like all others we indeed shall die.

Of Ashes and of Dirt
Tamiko Lemberger-Truelove

The day has died and in its demise birthed night.
The hours have emptied themselves into solemnity
And despair. Stars emerge from their graves of shadows
And broken light.

Years have fallen, and descended to an unfaltering plight of
scampering futures and intransigent pasts.

Doubt dreams of certainty as creation begins
To mold itself. Fecund oaths breed apostates.

What is this chaos that uncertainty and oblivion
Have engendered the world to?

In this moment, when clarity has been forced upon me,
I understand, intrinsically, who you are.

Through your presence it is I, who has been shattered,
and can no longer view heaven through fractured sight.

We are of ashes and of dirt
I sew my soul into your earth.
I will love what has been denied me.

    For

You are the needle,
You are the thread
That pierces my flesh, and binds my soul.

When there is nothing else…
You are religion.

Stranger
Nesreen (Alsoraimi) Frost

Decompress
Tangled webs unweaving in my head
Constricted breath escapes my chest
Days and weeks that mesh
Like candles that forget
Their shape
I lose my way again

One hand open
One hand closed
I make an effort
Then my engine slows
Black or white
Wrong or right
It's not that clear
So that we can't chose a side

Like a stranger
I'll close my eyes
I'll let you guide
I can't stay
I've always been this way
I'm a stranger
I'll float above
You'll feel me
Just momentarily

I am in need
Of something outside this field of energy
Blocking all their frequencies
Listen to these waves inside of me
I keep my face close to the ground
Holding onto this island that I found
Waging peace within
I shift and bend with every in and out
Taking what was always free
Everything chaotically

Beautiful
as it should be
The order I see
Is timeless and temporary
Makes you squirm in your seat
Takes you far away from me

Like a stranger
I'll close my eyes
I'll let you guide
I cannot stay
I've always been this way
I'm a stranger
I'll float above
You'll feel me
Just momentarily

The Addict
Juanita Ratner

No inner core
The doctor had said
Early on this child
Never allowed expression
Now masquerading
As an accomplished loving woman
Had learned
To abandon herself
To express what people wanted to hear
Needed
At least she was needed
But what a price
Never listening
To that voice within
Calling out in desperation

She fed it food
A little something pleasant
At least her senses
Momentarily
Knew some satisfaction
Others had their own ways
Food was so available
And somehow it did numb
That something
She couldn't face

But now her life is changing
No longer numb
Awakening moment by moment
First memories
And new ideas that challenged, touched some of those
Carefully protected zones
Healing balm of the Spirit
Felt deep in meditation
Working gently in the dim light
Unnoticed at first
Welcomed as the soothing waters of a gentle stream

So calming
So inviting
Until the "spirit rehydration program"
Stirred the life within this woozy listless soul.

She saw her beauty in the eyes of those around her
Found her power in the life she had somehow
Managed to carry on
Competently, lovingly
Despite her illness

But now a power within
Seeks that wholeness
Now that it is finding its voice
It seeks expression
Oneness
Truth
In her life

But that is hard
That takes work
And suffering
To see what really is

Often she still feels this fragile child
How can she remember
That though this child is also she
Still she is so much more

How can she connect with this beauty
She is for others
Own the intelligence so keen
It drove her underground
To escape the pain
Of the loneliness
Of seeing what others
Themselves couldn't face?
Allow the love that longs to pour out
Without allowing it to smother her own tender flame
Wavering when others are around
But yet burning inside with such intensity

That she can't pace herself.
She wants it all at once
Silence
Clarity
Perfect mother, family alive, in balance
Connectedness to the forces of her moment in time
Honesty
Friends
Love
Beauty
God
Stop!
Too much?
Sometimes it all swirls around inside
Where did the simplicity go?
Can it be found in wakefulness?
Can one be aware of so much at once
And not shatter
Or run to one's addiction,
And have calmness of spirit?

With something like
A timid boldness
She must both
Reach out
And wait
Open, yet focused
Feeling, yet not forgetting her wisdom
Learning new ways
Yet seeking the freshness
Of no patterns

The God of her acquaintance
Is many-faceted
The Tao that carries all
The Bread of Life that nourishes her human soul
The Savior who breaks into her patterns of soul-suicide
  with transforming love
The unnamable vastness behind all she can conceive
The oneness of a truth that has no otherness

The tear in her soul must mend
Into the oneness
Of the one seamless garment
Of divine thread
That clothes the universe
And contains herself and all within it.

Blend
Emily Lasinsky

Too dark to be light,
Too light to be dark,
Don't want to be either or.

I'm a blend, an integration of parts.
Some days the shadows mute the angels,
and other days my light blinds the bats.
I get along with the angels,
I get along with the bats,
We all talk about our need to take flight.
This is only a brief conversation.
After five minutes, the bats start to wither and
the angels start to remember being human.

Despite their strong persistence,
I resist the temptations the bats offer me,
especially in the form of hospitality,
the way they make me feel like family.
I know their intentions,
this sense of knowing is my angelic gift.
I curse the bats
in the dark
when they get jealous of my light.
They gather around me, feed my dark,
and I'm left in constant rumination,
questioning my existence.
Just then, Michael charges in with sword in hand and the bats know
their place.
No deal made, but an understanding.

I'm not going to avoid the dark,
but I want more Light to consume me.
Because I am Light, I can hang with the bats.
The angels call me to a higher standard,
but my white is ten shades off.
I'm not sure if I want to be brighter,
get rid of the stains of experience.

Help me to not resist Your Love,
Help me to persist in believing that the Light overpowers
the endless power outage that is the dark.
Help me to believe that this dark angel will be welcomed
and not merely exist in space
when she comes home.

Transcendence is Not the Way...
Candice Hershman

The moment when we see
the myth is our lives:
the moment when we see
our lives are the myth...
everything is luminous
with darkness.

Now I see
the insanity of transcendence.
I've recognized that pretty lies extend themselves
far beyond the guise of our most obvious adversaries:
that the guru's smile can sometimes be
just as fake as the politician's,
telling us that the way is so easy
if we just deny everything of who we are,
and we are not just a smile.
We are everything.

Everybody has darkness and light,
but when we use the mask of enlightenment
to dishonor the pain of other people,
to self elevate,
flying above the embodiment of suffering at a teasing distance,
then the bottom is up and the top is down.
It seems that those who
perpetuate the most pain
call this ignorance consciousness,
and pretend that being numb is bliss.
This is Lucifer,
the castaway.
He exiles himself with his self-righteousness,
living in his tower,
gripping tight to his wings
like a hoarder who is unknowingly
weighed down by his lightness.

The Bodhisattva stays,
just like Christ,

and knows that in order to truly know God,
he must know what it means first
to be a man.
He does not ascend with spiritual piety.
He does not avoid with intellectual conjecture.
He joins through the flesh
with feelings in his marrow,
embracing through entrance
into the place we thought to exile,
for the Garden did not leave us.
We left the Garden.
He cries,
envies, hates, grieves,
wishes and desires,
and knowing this to be everything,
he is closest to God.

Supplication
Katherine Kreil-Sarkar

A Dantean Homage

All our hearts are fragile mortal remnants.
Throbbing electric percussion
measurement of moments
Stars, jewels of the goddess
Divinia
In my chamber I lament unheard
Lady of all bitter mercies,
Love, aid thy feeble servant
Fallen asleep like a beaten sobbing child.
Lilies and other funeral flowers
Lullaby
How can I abide this treachery
Aching trembling heart
Burning in my hands, my chest
Torment winds blow me unbidden
I am whipped by winds of my own passion

I starve and there is no food
What would you have me eat? How
far into insanity shall i fall?
As I turn against you, I am against
my own self.
What horrors lie in store
as my flesh rots. You torture me
as I have breath in my body.
I blame you, I implore you.
This corporeal frailty constantly betrays me.

***

Parts of this poem were drawn phrases from Dante's *La Vita Nuova*.

The Dahlia
Nance Reynolds

Autumn scents arrive tonight,
  step in close to summer.
close enough to mingle together, in the breeze.

From across busy streets,
I glimpse the radiant beauty!
sparkling and alive, with a stature whispering of grace.
  My heart leaps beyond,
...as the moment fills with pause.

Darting with abandon through daily chaos,
Trusting the worth of this enticement,
      leaving behind whatever was taking my mind,
I settle here with you.

Now in close proximity, we speak.
Ahaha, you are here amidst all of this! me too!
 Crimson petals align in conical rhythm,
each sincerely devoted to her neighbor,
unified by evening light,
touching edges, creating second by second,
 a new palette.

Nowhere in my wildest dreams,
 ...did I think I would meet God tonight.

Eyes
Louis Hoffman

Her head lowered
as if to disappear into her hijab
gracefully covering her head
sinking as if into Allah

The man on the bus
leaned in toward her
small droplets of raging water
spewing from his lips
fists clenched at his side
"You're one of them,
a terrorist!
Go home!
Just go home!"

The woman pulls her young son close
one hand over his ear
hugging the other to her breast
protecting him from the violent vibrations
reverberating throughout the bus

Sitting at the back
watching
my heart is pounding in fear
'I should do something…'
Instead I look around
seeking cues

A group of youth
laugh callously

A man with dirty hands
after a long day's work
jaw clenched
nodded his approval

A couple sit uncomfortably
as if nothing was happening

Eyes averted
No one
acts

Rationales sprint through my thoughts:
'I have my own family'
'I will just make things worse by speaking up'
'What if others join in because I speak'
'He's not going to physically hurt them'
'I should just let it pass'
'It will be over soon'

Next stop
The woman quickly exits...
It was not her stop
I watch her on the street
anxiously looking to her surroundings
trying to figure what to do
where to go

Verses of sacred scriptures
spring into my thoughts
and now my head is the one that drops
disgraced and convicted
faith returning
only once fear is gone

Send-off
Robert A. Neimeyer

The dead linger around us,
stand at the shore
ready to push off
in their slow boats.
They finger the mooring line,
cast an eye to the sky
grey with rain. They feel
the ebb tide coming for them,
drawing them away
like forgetting.

They wait, patient as pilgrims,
for our thick hold to weaken,
arms to fall. They yearn to slip free
of the tight knot of our grief,
seek the silence beyond our piercing sobs.
They know in their bones
we will not lift the anchor,
hoist the sail. They bear the farewell
as a final duty.

We reach for their thin hands,
clutch their skirts, tug their sleeves.
We seek the refuge of their limp arms
as a ship steers toward harbor
in a storm. They hold our past
in their vacant eyes. Our future
is sealed behind their lips. We cannot bear
the endless present.

They sense the call to board their vessels
like the screech of distant gulls. They feel
the tremble in our fingers, hear
the gathering quiet
in our wracked gasps. They know
the months are doing their rhythmic work,
wearing us like waves. In the end
we will release them,

force a wan smile, raise an anxious palm

or join them in our time
to make the passage.

Invocation
Lorraine Mangione

if I can just stand in this center,
and walk a devout line to and from
two poles of shining beacon light,
and match my cadence to that of some
all-resounding hymn of the universe, pause,
        stand,
let whole body beat with the
driving blood of my heart,
blood of my grandmothers,
blood of hoary peaks and verdant plains,
and just walk,
with each step a closer view,
with each step the edges of the
world become clear;
(Someday I shall return here and fly;
  for now I walk with steps of order.)
and if this darkling incense spires
to all corners,
yet I stay in solemn ecstasy–
first at one great halo of
irridescence, sapphirine emeralds,
next at a point of flame
alive in a cave unentered,
then a dove shall come to rest,
and my chamber shall be all of light.

Here
Jyl Anais Ion

Here
is a rectangular styrofoam block,
broken, floating
on an ocean of despair,
of loneliness
and past betrayals,
an ocean, a wound full of tears
spread wide across a horizon.
Doubt is a river
of lost moments,
a time that never arrived.

Here
is the ugly crying face.
Here is the exhaustion.
Here is the not knowing
when I will ever feel better.

Here is a long road from where
I have been.

Here is lost.
Here is tearful.
Here is afraid.
Here is outspoken.
Here is unspoken.
Here is silent.
Here is aloud.

Here is unknown.

Here is breath.
Here is wind
and a promise of cold.
Here is a whisper
and a voice pointing home.

Here is the fear of remaining alone.

Equanimity
Bruce Elliot Alford

He lifts his hands and remembers the Host taken on First nights, those stories, songs and Sunday school verses he learned. *Train up a child in the way he should go and when he is old, he will not depart ....*

After noon, people pour onto the street. Women show off their hats, such wondrous blossoms. Two and two walk together, leaving the Lord's House.

O-oh, he sees himself so near now—*have mercy lord*—in his little suit and tie, wearing glistening shoes, thinking he will be somebody. His faith is too beautiful and cruel. *Immanuel*, the earth is full of beauty, cruelty, boundless love and ritual killing.

How can a man bring the two together? It is not so simple to find no contradiction in union. Almost abruptly, his affection for the master turns to bitterness. Yet somehow he lights a candle and goes to silence, which is charitable. Silence knows incandescence. Silence knows what is best.

Not to ask for anything. This is sacred.

When a Student is Ready
Wade Agnew

During a time of profound inner peace,
joy for no reason at all
or from allowing
nothing to hinder it
and this was my natural state, like some people say.

In a steam room perfectly content
sitting on tile alone
lacking nothing,
anticipating nothing, regretting nothing;
thinking of nothing,

feeling joy

A woman and nearly five year old enter,
acknowledging their arrival
just enough
to be aware of their presence
choosing not
to be distracted,
drawing back
to being
satisfied with nothing.

When out of silence came a question
from the young girl
spoken clearly, directly, sincerely, while looking straight at me.

"Are you an angel?"

Hearing as well as
listening
to the question.
Noticing the mind noticing
how quickly
we bought into calling ourselves human beings
with its limited boundaries,

that have been
created and accepted.

Repeating the question
to myself... am I?
I felt the expansion of joy
from her inquiry,
it speaking
to greatness beyond people who practice it.

She asked so powerfully.

I could not answer,
different things came, none
worthy of saying
in a pause that
allowed
plenty of time for an answer.

She was patient, staying attentive
even when mother
wrapped arms
around shoulder
pulling her in saying, "Ah honey... no."

Attempting to sooth
embarrassment
that was not there.

A teaching of play it safe
masqueraded as,
being loving,
molding
conditioned,
limited, closed minded
thinking into place.

Probably we were both responsible.

The young girl so beautiful.
Thank you.
I know myself better.

***

"When a Student is Ready" was previously published in Haight Asbury Literary Journal, Volume 27, Number 1 and the book *Solace for a Starving, Naked, Alone in the Dark* Soul by Wade Agnew.

Appendix
Poetry Activities

In the appendix, we introduce a number of exercises that can be used to deepen your understanding of your spiritual journey, hopefully leading to healing and growth. Additionally, they may be helpful in growing as a poet. Many of these activities can be done individually or in groups. You may consider using them as part of a group that meets regularly, with a friend, or in conjunction with counseling, therapy, or spiritual direction.

Exercise 1: Creating a Spiritual Metaphor
Spend some time reflecting upon what might be a good metaphor for your spiritual journey. Try not to rush to the first metaphor that comes to mind. Instead, allow yourself to meditate on this and consider many possibilities. You may want to write down various ones you consider along the way. After you have selected your metaphor, see if you can develop this into a poem. This activity can be done individually or in groups.

Exercise 2: Spiritual Path Poem
The Divine Comedy (Inferno, Purgitorio, and Paradiso) by Dante Alighieri is likely the most famous poetry on spiritual struggles of all time. In this epic poem, Dante tells a fictional story of the journey through hell and purgatory to paradise. In this activity, imagine your own spiritual journey as a path or a trip. Write a poem about this journey trying to incorporate as much symbolism as you can that represents your spiritual experiences along the way. It does not need to be as long as *The Divine Comedy*! This activity can be done individually or in groups.

Exercise 3: Poetic Meditations
Meditation is common in spiritual traditions; however, there are many types of meditation. In this exercise, we are referring to a reflective type of meditation. Set aside 15-30 minutes a day for a period of time. Begin your meditation by creating a context conducive to self-reflection. Generally, it is best to have a place that is quiet and free from distraction. Begin your meditation by reading one of the

poems from this book. With some poems, it may be helpful to read the poem a couple of times. Use the poem as a springboard for meditating. The intent is not to meditate on understanding the poem, but rather to see where the poem takes you in your own reflections.

For some, journaling may be your best approach to reflection or meditation, while for others it may work best to sit silently with your thoughts. At the end of the time, try writing your own poem.

We encourage you to make this a ritual for a period of time. You may even decide to work through the entire book this way, reading a poem a day.

Exercise 4: Poetry to God or the Sacred
Take a moment to reflect upon what you consider to be the sacred, whether this is God, nature, the universe, or something entirely different. Consider what you would like to communicate to God or the sacred, and then write a poem (or letter) attempting to communicate what you would like to say. Particularly if going through a period of spiritual transition, it can be helpful to revise the poem over time, keeping each version, or to write a series of poems over time and observe how they change. Reflecting upon the change can be a powerful source of adding insight into your spiritual journey. The time frame for the revisions or poems in the series can be anywhere from several weeks to several years.

Exercise 5: Poem from God or the Sacred
In this exercise, compose a poem to yourself or about yourself from God or the sacred. You may consider writing one based upon how you feel the relationship to be currently and one based upon how you would like the relationship to be. This can be done individually or in groups.

Exercise 6: Dialogue with God or the Sacred
This exercise is a combination of exercises 4 and 5. Through poetry (or letters), have a dialogue between yourself and God or the sacred. This can extend as long as you would like, and can be done individually or in groups. If used in groups, it is recommended to have the exercise in advance so that the poems can be written prior to meeting.

Appendix 191

Exercise 7: Poetry of God or the Sacred
In *Pastoral Care of Depression*, Moriarty (2006) encourages people to draw a picture of God. Often, the picture can produce insights into one's thoughts about God. In this activity, instead of drawing a picture of God, try writing a poem describing God or the sacred. The poem can highlight images, qualities, feelings, and other aspects of what you associate with God or the sacred. Alternatively, you may begin by drawing a picture of God or the sacred and follow this by writing a poem. This exercise can be done individually or in groups.

Moriarty, G. (2006). *Pastoral care of depression: Helping clients heal their relationship with god.* New York, NY: Haworth Pastoral Press.

Exercise 8: Hearing Differently*
Divide into groups of 3-6 people, preferably through a random selection. Each member will write a poem expressing his or her spiritual journey. After the poems have been completed, pass them to the person to the right. Choose someone to begin reading their poem. After each reading, allow at least 20-30 seconds of silence, then discuss the experience of the poem (e.g., what each person thought, emotionally felt, physically felt). Avoid debating the meaning or critiquing of any kind. After everyone has had a chance to give his or her reflection, have the original author read the poem again. After another period of silence, have the group again reflect on their experience and reactions. The purpose of this activity is to share collaboratively both individual and collective experiences about how spirituality is uniquely expressed and experienced. Use the following discussion points to guide further discussion (if needed):

1. What have you learned from this exercise?
2. How might this new insight change the way you support the spiritual journey of others?
3. How might insights change the way your approach your own spiritual journey?

* This activity is based upon an activity in *Capturing Shadows: Poetic Encounters Along the Path of Grief and Loss* by Louis Hoffman and Michael Moats, published in 2016 by University Professors Press.

Exercise 9: Themes
Take time to read all of the poems. You can do this in one sitting or several. As you are reading mark those poems that touch you most deeply. Do not worry about how many you mark; simply focus on which poems have the most significant influence on you emotionally and spiritually. Once you have done this, go back and re-read those poems you marked and choose the five that emerge as the having the greatest impact on you.

Over the next week (maybe even two) re-read each of these five poems and journal the thoughts, reflections, concepts, emotions, and questions each of these poems generates for you. Be as specific as you can. Allow yourself a block of time each day to do this (not less than 15 minutes and as much as an hour if that is possible).

Once you have completed this period of re-reading the poems and journaling, walk away from the poems and your journaling for at a least week. Do not look at what you have written or add any additional entries. Simply leave it alone.

After one week, come back to your journal entries and read them. In fact, re-read them several times to identify themes that appear in your entries. For some these themes may emerge quickly, but for many this will require several re-readings of the entries. Generally, the more times you review your entries the clearer the themes will become. Focus on pinpointing two or three primary themes.

Now that you have ascertained the primary themes, spend some time reflecting on the following questions:

1. Which of the themes, if any, are surprising to you? In what way do they surprise you?
2. How have these themes been evident in your life (think of past experiences or moments in your life when these themes have been present)?
3. How are these themes influencing your life currently (relationships, career, self-perception, spiritual practices, etc.)?
4. How might your acknowledgement of and reflection on these themes help you as you move forward with life spiritually? Emotionally? Psychologically? Relationally?

Consider sharing what you are learning from this experience with a trusted friend or mentor. Perhaps even involve that person in assisting you with clarifying and focusing the themes that are emerging for you.

Other Books by University Professors Press
www.universityprofessorspress.com

Stay Awhile: Poetic Narratives on Multiculturalism and Diversity
By Louis Hoffman & Nathaniel Granger, Jr.

Capturing Shadows: Poetic Encounters Along the Path of Grief & Loss
By Louis Hoffman & Michael Moats

Psychotherapy's Pilgrim-Poet: The Story Within
By Betsy Hall

The Polarized Mind: Why It's Killing Us and What We Can Do About It
By Kirk Schneider

Bare: Psychotherapy Stripped
By Jacqueline Simon Gunn & Carlo DeCarlo

Humanistic Contributions for Psychology 101: Growth, Choice, and Responsibility
By Richard Bargdill & Rodger Broomé

An Artist's Thought Book: Intriguing Thoughts About the Artistic Process
By Richard Bargdill

The Buddha, the Bike, the Couch, and the Circle: A Festschrift for Dr. Robert Unger
By Michael M. Dow, Francis J. Kaklauskas, & Elizabeth Olson

Love Outraged and the Liberation of the Core Self
By Franklin Sollars

Our Last Walk: Using Poetry for Grieving and Remembering Our Pets
By Louis Hoffman, Michael Moats, and Tom Greening (Summer, 2016)

About the Editors

Louis Hoffman, PhD, is a faculty member at Saybrook University and serves as the director of the Existential, Humanistic, and Transpersonal Psychology Specialization. He also teaches in the Creativity Studies program at Saybrook, and teaches two courses on poetry: Poetry, Healing, and Growth, and The Use of Poetry with Death, Loss, and Life Transitions. In 2016, he was appointed as a fellow of the American Psychological Association and the Society for Humanistic Psychology for his contributions to the field of psychology. Dr. Hoffman has seven prior books, including *Stay Awhile: Poetic Narratives on Multiculturalism and Diversity*, *Capturing Shadows: Poetic Encounters Along the Path of Grieving and Loss*, and *Spirituality and Psychological Health*. In addition to his academic work, Dr. Hoffman is a licensed psychologist and maintains a therapy practice in Colorado Springs, Colorado. One of his clinical emphases is working with clients who are struggling with religious and spiritual issues. Most importantly, however, Dr. Hoffman is a husband and a father. He lives with his wife, three sons, and their dog, Dante, in beautiful Colorado Springs, Colorado.

Steve Fehl, PsyD, is a bereavement educator and grief counselor. Previous writing projects have included being a regular contributor to *The New Existentialist* blog, as well as a contributing co-author of chapters in *Unearthing The Moment*; *Explaining Evil*; *Existential Psychology East–West*; *Miracles: God, Psychology, and Science in the Paranormal*; and *Whole Person Health Care*. In addition, Steve serves on the Editorial Board of *University Professors Press*. Prior to earning his doctorate in clinical psychology at the University of the Rockies in 2011, Steve served Lutheran parishes in Texas, Michigan, California, Minnesota, and Colorado. His clinical interests include faith and spirituality; spiritual abuse; existential theology; the role of spirituality in existential psychology; bereavement and grief; as well as Lesbian, Gay, Bisexual, and Transgender (LGBT) issues. Steve lives in Colorado Springs, Colorado with his wife, Chris, and two dachshunds – Jed and Gracie.

www.ingramcontent.com/pod-product-compliance
Lightning Source LLC
Chambersburg PA
CBHW070611170426
43200CB00012B/2657